Great Cathedrals

Great Cathedrals

Plantagenet Somerset Fry

Crescent Books
New York

Photographic acknowledgments

Agerpress, Bucharest 102; Alinari, Florence 11 top, 83, 87, 90–91; Archives Photographiques, Paris 30; Belgian National Tourist Office, London 43, 44; E. Boudot-Lamotte, Paris 86, 106; Brazilian Embassy, London 123; British Tourist Authority, London 15, 20, 22, 23 top, 23 bottom, 29 top, 29 bottom; J. Allan Cash, London 6, 13, 41, 42, 45, 48, 68, 71, 73, 84, 93; Cathedral Church of St John the Divine, New York City 112, 113; Colour Library International, London 9, 17, 21, 24, 25, 40, 49, 65 top, 82 top, 85 bottom, 88–89, 115, 116, 117, 120, 121, 124, 125 bottom; Courtauld Institute, London 27 left; Danish Tourist Board, London 63, 64 top; Embassy of Peru, London 126; German National Tourist Office, London 51, 58, 59 left; Photographie Giraudon, Paris 7 bottom, 35, 70; Sonia Halliday, Weston Turville 8, 56 bottom; Hamlyn Group Picture Library back cover, endpapers, 11 bottom, 16 bottom, 28, 32, 33, 34, 36, 37, 38 left, 38 right, 39, 50 top left, 50 top right, 50 bottom, 85 top, 92, 114, 122; Hirmer Fotoarchiv, Munich 103 bottom; Michael Holford, Loughton front cover, title spread; A. F. Kersting, London 7 top, 12, 14 left, 19, 26, 31, 54, 55, 56 top left, 56 top right, 61, 78, 81, 82 bottom, 94 right, 95; Bildarchiv Foto Marburg, Marburg Lahn 10, 27 right, 91, 99 right; M.A.S., Barcelona 72, 74, 75 left, 75 right, 77, 79; Marion Morrison, Woodbridge 125 top; Netherlands National Tourist Office, London 46, 47; Novosti Press Agency, London 107, 110, 111; Picturepoint, London 118; Portuguese National Tourist Office, London 80; Josephine Powell, Rome 103 top; Jean Roubier, Paris 14 right; St Mary's Cathedral, San Francisco 119; Tony Stone Associates, London 65, 76; Swedish National Tourist Office, London 66, 67; Swiss National Tourist Office, London 62; Roger Viollet, Paris 59 right; Werner Forman Archive, London 99 left; Woodmansterne, Watford 16 top; Yugoslav National Tourist Office, London 94 left; ZEFA, London 52, 53, 57 left, 57 right, 60, 64 bottom, 69, 96, 97, 98, 100, 101, 104, 105, 108, 109.

The ground plan on page 127 is reproduced from *The Architecture of Europe* by Doreen Yarwood (B. T. Batsford, London, 1974); that on page 128 from *Cathedrals of Europe* by Ann Mitchell (Paul Hamlyn, Feltham, 1968).

Front cover:	Salisbury Cathedral, England
Back cover:	Notre-Dame, Paris, France
Endpapers:	Bourges Cathedral, France
Title spread:	Florence Cathedral, Italy

First English edition published by
The Hamlyn Publishing Group Limited
London · New York · Sydney · Toronto
Astronaut House, Feltham, Middlesex, England

Library of Congress Catalog Card Number: 82-71418

This edition is published by Crescent Books
Distributed by Crown Publishers, Inc.
h g f e d c b a
Printed in Italy

CONTENTS

Introduction

In the Middle Ages, Christianity filled people's lives and the church was the most important building in any community in Europe. Today we are still astonished at the remarkable buildings our ancestors raised to the glory of God, which remain for us to admire and perhaps to learn from. The greatest of these were the cathedrals – hundreds of them from western Scotland and Ireland to central Russia, from northern Norway to Sicily and Athens. Many of them were gigantic *tours de force* of uncomplicated masons, who created what they believed to be microcosms of Heaven, or symbols of the mystical body of God's only son, Jesus Christ. Today they still dominate the landscape (like Segovia in Spain), the skyline (Ely in England) and the city (Prague in Czechoslovakia). Even when they are small, like Christ Church in Oxford or Little Metropole in Athens, they still impress with their sacred aura and their lovely architecture. How much more vast, spatial and awe-inspiring so many of them must have seemed to medieval people, when they were so often the largest buildings anywhere in the country.

A cathedral is a church that contains a bishop's throne. The word comes from the Greek καθεδρα (*kathedra*) which means 'seat', and the throne is generally to be found by a cathedral's choir stalls. The area over which a bishop presides is known as a see, which also means 'seat', from the Latin *sedes*. Very early in Christian history it was decided that a bishop's cathedral church should be in a town or city within the boundaries of his see. In mainland Europe this presented few difficulties because there were numerous towns and cities, but in Britain there were few towns of any size before the 11th century, and there are instances of bishoprics not centred on any place but rather migratory, that is, the cathedra was in one church, then in another. There was, for example, a bishop of the South Saxons, another for the West Saxons, and so forth.

The fortunes of cathedrals varied: some lost their status; many were rebuilt, a few several times; many have been attacked in war or vandalized in revolutionary movements; many endured structural collapse

The great south-west tower of Segovia is an austere feature of this otherwise ornate cathedral, noted for its pinnacles and its warm, golden stone.

Left: The Octagon with its lantern at Ely, one of the most original designs of the 14th century, was dedicated in the presence of Edward III and his queen, Philippa of Hainault.

through storms or through faulty building. Many were started, left for decades, some even for centuries, and then completed. More often than not this was because the money ran out. And indeed, hardly any cathedrals were finished in less than 100 years.

A cathedral was managed by its chapter, a body of priests headed by a dean, or in the case of cathedrals associated with monasteries (where the abbot was also the bishop), a body of monks. The chapter was responsible for building the cathedral in the first place and for maintaining it thereafter. Although the individual members died or moved on, there was a continuity that ensured that sooner or later the cathedral would be finished, and even after centuries of work there was always an instantly discernible unity in the design, whether it was of one main style or a combination of styles.

Once it had been decided to build a new cathedral, or enlarge and modify an existing one – and the majority of cathedrals in this book are second or third buildings – the chapter chose one of their own number as project manager, who would also look after the finances. In the Middle Ages (roughly 800–1500), when the great majority of cathedrals were

begun, the clergy were almost the only people who understood how to manage such projects, some of them having had experience on other sites or learned from visits to projects in other countries. The canon in charge looked around for a suitable architect. The term is used to embrace the skills, not the qualifications, since in the Middle Ages they did not exist in the academic sense. He would be a stonemason with a high reputation and proven experience. In many instances he would be invited from another country. He might bring with him one or two assistants whose work he trusted.

The architect hired his team of master craftsmen, masons, sculptors, carpenters, stonecutters, blacksmiths, glass-makers, tilers, brick-makers, cement-mixers and quarrymen, who were accompanied by assistants and sometimes apprentices. There would also be an army of labourers drawn from the city and its surroundings. Each master set up his own timber-built workshop on site. A drawing of the building of a church tower, by Jan van Eyck and dating from about 1437, shows the masons' lodge as a lean-to against the tower wall, with sharply sloping roof to deflect falling masonry.

The architect prepared plans which he produced in a bed of

Building a church tower in the 15th century. In the foreground is a portrait of St Barbara, to whom the church is dedicated. Note the lean-to on the right for the masons.

Christ Pantocrator in mosaic looks sternly down from the ceiling of the great crossing dome at Alexander Nevski Cathedral in Sofia.

plaster or on a sheet of wood (and later in the Middle Ages on parchment, and later still on paper). They consisted of a ground plan and an elevation; the additional details were worked out as the construction proceeded. When the chapter approved, work began on clearing the site and marking out the eastern end. The eastern end was almost always started first (though at Amiens it was the nave) because the high altar had to be placed in the east to catch the rising sun, which was seen symbolically as Christ, the Son of God, rising after the darkness of the crucifixion. The building works moved westwards.

Simultaneously with setting out, master carpenters with their work force went to the nearest forest to fell, trim and collect timber for scaffolding, cranes, windlasses and great wheels, while master quarrymen and their force hacked out the stone at the nearest quarries, or sometimes further away, and cut it to shapes determined by special templates. Each stone was marked to indicate its position in the structure, and also to identify the quarryman and the cutter, so that they would get paid. Back at the site, diggers excavated the foundation trenches, and then the bishop, or someone of similar status, was invited to lay the foundation stone. Sometimes the cathedral would be dedicated at this point to its particular patron saint.

The different designs and styles of cathedral architecture are the subject of a vast and interesting literature, and we can only summarize the ideas here. Cathedrals were first built on the basilican plan. A *basilica* was a Roman hall of justice and administration, characterized by its rectangular plan, about twice as long as wide, with two or four rows of columns down the longer axis to make aisles, and with a rounded apsidal end where the tribunal sat. The ceiling was flat and the roof gabled. Entry was at the end opposite the apse, and in Christian basilicas part of that end consisted of an entrance chamber, or narthex, which had an arcaded porch.

The basilica was adapted over the earlier centuries of Christianity throughout Europe in a variety of forms. In the Eastern Roman Empire they were often adorned with a dome over the centre, some having smaller domes and half-domes surrounding it or elsewhere on the roof line. The dome was intended to symbolize the vault of Heaven, and would generally be decorated with a mosaic picture of Christ Pantocrator (Creator of all things). This dome theme spread into later Russian cathedrals where the domes assumed distinctive shapes, such as the famous 'onion tops'. Eastern basilicas gave way to the Greek-cross plan (a church built on a cross with arms of equal length), but in the West, basilica churches continued to be raised and are still built today. There was another early style, the 'mausoleum', built on a concentric double circle or double polygon plan carrying a central dome. The original work of the Palatine Chapel of Charlemagne at Aachen Cathedral is a good 9th-century example.

After the collapse of the Western Roman Empire in the late 5th century, western Europeans began to pick themselves up much sooner than has often been supposed; the Dark Ages is fast becoming a mythical and not an actual period. Christianity survived in isolated areas and was carried along by devoted scholars and monks, chiefly from Ireland, Italy and France. Places of worship were built, or grafted on to older Roman Christian structures, and there emerged what we call the Romanesque style, which is generally dated in Western Europe from about 600 to about 1200. It has two phases, the pre-Romanesque (including Carolingian) and the Romanesque.

At first, Romanesque followed ancient Roman principles, with

The bizarre and colourful cathedral of St Basil the Blessed in Red Square, Moscow, begun by Ivan the Terrible in the mid-16th century.

The octagonal interior of the Palatine Chapel at Aachen Cathedral which is one of the earliest surviving church buildings in Europe.

the emphasis on proportion, the use of round-headed arches and solid columns. Then architects began to experiment with vaulting. Arches were built to spring out of column capitals to provide a ribbed framework for a vaulted ceiling. This scheme was applied to basilicas, but it was also tried out with the relatively new cruciform style of building, using the Latin cross in which the western (nave) arm is longer than the other three. At first, the arches were rounded, but the pointed arch, an innovation reaching Europe as a result of contact with the Saracenic Arabs, reduced the outward thrust of a

vault. Romanesque architects also introduced the flying buttress, an arched prop designed to counter outward thrust. When the innovations were put together in one architectural scheme, the Gothic style can be said to have arrived, and this was pioneered in France.

The Gothic style pervaded ecclesiastical architecture in Europe from about 1100 right through to the 16th century. Every country was influenced, and each expressed its conception of it in an individual manner, at the same time retaining the broad essentials so superbly demonstrated in the Gothic

Above: The magnificently fortress-like Romanesque cathedral of Cefalù, in Sicily. Note the pilaster buttresses clamped round the north transept and along the eastern arm, a Norman castle feature.

Left: The wide Galilee porch at Durham serves as the cathedral's Lady Chapel. Lady Chapels are usually at the east end, but this one is said to have been sited at the west end because St Cuthbert disliked women!

11

cathedrals built in the Ile de France between the mid-12th century and the end of the 14th, namely, Laon, Notre-Dame (Paris), Chartres, Reims and Amiens.

The Gothic can be summarized, if inadequately, as a style which strove to reach up to Heaven, signified by soaring heights, floating space and a unique combination of stretching and balancing of materials and forms. Walls gave way to buttresses, vertical spaces were filled with stained glass to symbolize the Light of God, 'ever changing as it passes through images of events in the life of Christ and His saints'. Shafts shot upwards from column capitals into vaults that seemed to defy the laws of gravity. Western fronts, pierced by bold, recessed portals, were covered with decorative sculpture, and flanked by massive, thrusting towers and spires rising to unprecedented heights. Stone was used and shaped in a multitude of exciting new ways. It was a period characterized by almost daemonic building energy and unceasing experiment.

Gothic was to be replaced gradually by the styles of the Renaissance, a movement towards the individualization of man, away from hierarchical Christianity. This was manifest in a return to pure classical forms, notably those in architecture that were rediscovered after centuries of obscurity. It began in the late 14th century in Italy, and was given a significant boost when the manuscripts of the Roman engineer-architect Marcus Vitruvius Pollio (flourished *c.* 30 B.C.–*c.*15 A.D.) were discovered. The pioneering changes of the

Daylight illuminates the stained glass of the nave and west end of the French Gothic 'coronation' cathedral of Reims.

The west doorway to the tiny Little Metropole cathedral in Athens, by far the smallest cathedral in the world.

Italians spread throughout Europe and, as with the Gothic, produced highly individual manifestations in each country. The Renaissance in turn generated a reaction to its insistence on classical truth, and this was the Baroque, most cogently illustrated by the use of strong curves and diagonals in decorative sculpture, a picturesque style of the 17th and 18th centuries.

Up to the 11th century, cathedrals were small by comparison with what followed, though St Sophia's in Istanbul was one gigantic exception. Then, as cities became more prosperous through increasing trade and commerce they expanded, and larger cathedrals were built. The cathedral was also assuming a much wider role in the community. The predominating religious function developed as worship became more elaborate, needing more altars and chapels, and these were provided in extended east ends, radiating chapels, and chapels between buttresses and along the walls of transepts. This function was to be shared with an increasing variety of other functions. The cathedral acted as a town hall, meeting place for craft guilds and assembly hall for academic functions, and it accommodated sittings of law courts, provided space for markets and fairs, and even put on plays. Cathedral crypts were increasingly used as sick bays. New and rebuilt cathedrals were often designed to accommodate a whole town: Amiens, for example, was geared to house 10,000 people, while today Ely would probably have enough room for the city's present population.

The growing division between religious and secular functions led

cathedral authorities to mark the gap in a structural sense, keeping and often enlarging the eastern end for themselves and separating it with a rood screen of wood, stone or iron, or a more substantial structure, the pulpitum, sometimes two or three metres (yards) thick, with doors. Some of these spoiled the vistas in cathedrals, and where they have been removed in subsequent generations it has usually been to the advantage of the spatial grandeur of the interior. At the same time, to provide the space for the secular functions, the nave was built longer and sometimes wider, with additional aisles. These and other needs were reflected in the designs and the spatial developments that are illustrated in this book. And as cathedrals were still – and always will be – primarily raised to the glory of God, they warranted the highest constructive and decorative skills obtainable. This alone accounts for the unending variety to be found in the architecture, sculpture and decoration of cathedrals. No two are alike, although some comparisons can be made, especially where it is known that particular distinguished artists and craftsmen or their pupils worked on more than one cathedral. Some of the better known names in the long roll call of leading medieval and Renaissance artists and craftsmen are included in the Glossary as well as mentioned in the text.

If one had to sum up the place of cathedrals in the story of Christian civilization, they are the supreme expression of that civilization's architecture and visual art, wherever they may be.

Above left: Rising to 43 metres (140 feet) – amongst the tallest in France – the nave and choir of Amiens rest upon marvellously slender clustered-shaft columns.

Above: The tremendous carved stone screen in front of the choir at Toledo Cathedral is a superb example of Spanish Gothic artistic craftsmanship.

Cathedrals of the British Isles

Coventry

On the night of 14 November 1940, Nazi German bombers destroyed the 14th-century cathedral of St Michael in an air raid on Coventry, leaving only the outer walls and tower and spire standing. The very next day it was decided that the cathedral would be rebuilt, and soon after the war the reconstruction committee invited designs from architects by competition. It was agreed not to rebuild the old cathedral but to build anew, right next door, and today visitors to the new can take a few steps to the side to walk round the gaunt shell of the old. The winning design was by Basil (later Sir Basil) Spence, and in June 1954 work began. Eight years later, his unusual, imaginative – and at the time highly controversial – cathedral was completed and consecrated.

Spence broke away from earlier more conventional styles, seeing that his cathedral should be a major representative of vigorous modern British architecture. It contains most of the usual features but they are arranged in an interestingly and often arrestingly new manner, using modern materials and techniques. Spence fully grasped the superimportance of illumination, and his disposition of windows and the coruscation of colour they produce more than compensate for the lack of the more traditional aspects one might hope to find.

The plan is a long, narrowish rectangle, on a north to south axis, with the high altar towards the north. The nave occupies a far greater proportion of the cathedral than in cruciform plans. The ceiling is a canopy of wood panelling resting upon a concrete grid supported by slim, tapering columns. Along each side of the nave are five splendid windows set at angles so that the light is

Graham Sutherland's remarkable Christ in Glory, probably the biggest tapestry in the world, dominates the interior of Coventry Cathedral.

thrown upon the high altar and the Lady Chapel behind it. Behind the Lady Chapel on the north wall hangs a tremendous tapestry of Christ in Glory, probably the biggest tapestry in the world, which replaces what would normally be an 'east' window. This is the fine work of Graham Sutherland, and it was woven near Aubusson in France. The tapestry aroused a storm of controversy when it was first revealed, but there is no doubt of its power and feeling. It is 22 metres (74 feet) high, 12 metres (38 feet) wide, and weighs over 900 kilograms (2000 pounds).

To the east of the Lady Chapel is the very small Chapel of Christ in Gethsemane, in which there is a finely sculptured screen of ironwork in the form of a crown of thorns. Also on the east side, but towards the south end, is the Baptistery, which has an amazing curved window 25 metres (81 feet) high and 15 metres (51 feet) across, and stretching from ground to ceiling. Designed by John Piper, it contains 195 slim, vertical lights of the most glorious stained glass which depict the patterns of Man's life through many-coloured representations. In front of the window inside stands the font, a hunk of Palestinian rock from the Valley of Barakat near Bethlehem, which has been carved out on the top to produce a bowl.

The south end of the cathedral is a vast wall of clear glass, decorated by John Hutton with etchings of angels, prophets and apostles. At ground level are three glass doors into St Michael's Porch, a covered way that is joined to the old cathedral. To the right of the eastern steps leading up to the porch is Epstein's heroic bronze sculpture of St Michael and the Devil which is mounted upon the sensitive pink sandstone of the cathedral fabric.

Above: The great Baptistery window, with nearly 200 lights, illuminates the nave of Coventry Cathedral in superb 'technicolour'.

Below: Where the old meets the new. The huge porch of new Coventry Cathedral hangs over the ruined shell of the old St Michael's Cathedral.

New Coventry Cathedral is very different from the old, but whichever way the visitor approaches, whether by going into the old shell first and then into the new building, or the other way round, the contrast seems not to intrude upon the much more dominant feeling of rebirth and reconciliation that Spence was aiming to embody in his architectural message.

Durham

It is impossible not to be overawed by the tremendously powerful aspect of Durham's monastery-cathedral, perched high on a steep rock over the river Wear. Whether you see it from the railway bridge spanning the river valley not far to the west or from any point in Durham city, the effect is awe-inspiring. In medieval times, it would have been forbidding too, for Durham Cathedral was a fortress as well as a monastery and church, and the

castle was an integral part of the buildings. It was the 'citadel' of the powerful bishops of Durham, who were counts palatine and lords of the North, delegated to govern there by the kings.

There was a cathedral at Durham in Saxon times. It had been built to house the relics of St Cuthbert and to provide a tomb for pilgrimage. Today that tomb is marked by a grey slab behind the high altar. The earlier building was presumably demolished, for no trace remains. Then, in the reign of William II (1087–1100), a new cathedral began to rise on the site, under the aegis of Bishop William de St Carilef. It was to be a splendid Norman-Romanesque structure on cruciform plan, with important architectural innovations, most notably the quadripartite ribbed vaulting of the huge nave and aisles, the choir with its aisles, and the transepts, said to be among the earliest such vaultings

One of the most arresting ecclesiastical sights in England, the tremendous western end of Durham Cathedral, suspended over the river Wear.

in Europe. The choir vaulting was altered in the 13th century.

Durham's nave is the dominant feature of the interior and it was completed by the 1130s. Over 60 metres (200 feet) long, it is flanked by two rows of magnificent columns variously decorated with chevron, fluted or diapered surfaces supporting a fine triforium, and above that the clerestory (which still has its original windows), the columns alternating with compound piers supporting the vault. Over the crossing is a central tower, 66 metres (218 feet) tall, in Perpendicular style, partly a rebuild of an original lower tower, in the 15th century. Much of the choir is the oldest part of the cathedral (late 11th century) with embellishment of later generations, particularly the fine

pinnacled altar screen of stone, installed by Lord Neville of Raby, a powerful Northumbrian baron, in the 1370s.

At the eastern end was added in the 13th century a pair of transepts in the form of a composite of nine small bays, known as the Chapel of the Nine Altars. This has a rose window (restored in the 18th century) which with the lancet lights helps to give the interior of Durham much more light than one might expect in a Norman cathedral, where the tendency was to overdo the size of column and pier and wall area in the interests of compensating for stress.

The western end has two towers whose upper storeys were completed in the early 13th century. In front of the west façade was added in the 1170s

The interior of England's largest Lady Chapel, at Ely, whose tall and wide windows were once filled with glorious stained glass.

the unusual Galilee porch, with five parallel aisles, separated by arcades of round-head arches decorated in sharp zigzag style supported on clusters of four very slender columns. In the Galilee is the tomb of the Venerable Bede (673–735), the great Anglo-Saxon scholar and historian who lived, worked and died at nearby Jarrow.

Ely

By any standards the outer aspect of Ely Cathedral is stunning – whether you see it from many miles away on Newmarket Heath or come upon it suddenly as you enter the city from the north or west. Its sheer size – it is all of 164 metres (537 feet) in length – is enhanced by the smallness of the city over which it towers, giving one an idea, perhaps better than in any other place, of what a medieval cathedral city was like in its heyday.

There had been a monastery on the site since the 670s, when it was founded by St Etheldreda. It endured fluctuating fortunes, being sacked by the Vikings in 869 but neglected thereafter for generations. The appointment of a Norman abbot soon after the Conquest opened a new chapter, and in 1083 the abbot began to build a great abbey church. Up went rows of massive Norman pillars to support three tiers of round-headed arches for a fine 12-bay nave that rises to a height of 26 metres (86 feet), the tallest Norman nave in England, finished in the 1130s. By 1106 the choir and central tower had been completed, and three years later Ely became a cathedral when its abbot became a bishop. Transepts, eastern and western, were built later in the century, the western receiving a single central tower (whose north-west arm collapsed in the 15th century and was never replaced). Between 1239 and 1250 the choir was extended, and the lovely western Galilee Porch was added to the door in the west tower.

In 1320, after a lengthy interval, the Lady Chapel was begun on the east corner of the north transept by the sacrist and engineer, Alan of Walsingham. But in 1322 disaster struck. The Norman tower in the centre of the cathedral fell down. The supporting pillars had been infilled with rubble instead of being solid and had given way. Alan of Walsingham seized the opportunity to erect in its place one of the most famous cathedral features in England, the Octagon.

Taking the breadth of the cathedral, including the aisles, for his base, and then cutting off the angles from the resultant square, he produced an octagon 23 metres (74 feet) across. Such a width could not be spanned in stone at that time, so he led his vaulting to the edge of it and devised a wooden lantern, or tower, to reach upwards from it. After much searching, eight straight oak trees large enough to yield timbers the necessary 19 metres (63 feet) long, 1 metre (3 feet 4 inches) wide and 0.8 metres (2 feet 8 inches) thick, were found in Bedfordshire and brought, like all the cathedral's building material, by boat to Ely. A leading master carpenter, William Hurley, raised these enormous timbers (which he had cased in lead sheet) to the roof and gave the cathedral the Octagon and Lantern, its crowning glory. In the 1340s he completed the interrupted work on the Lady Chapel, the biggest in England, having the widest medieval stone vault, at 14 metres (46 feet).

Stepping into the cathedral, one has a breathtaking view, for Ely has no stone screen to separate monks from laity, as most cathedrals have. It is colourful, too, for two Victorian gentlemen spent about 17 years on their backs in the scaffolding, painting the wooden roof of the nave.

Perfect geometry in the vault of the Octagon at Ely Cathedral.

Above: St Paul's Cathedral was damaged in air raids on London during the Second World War, particularly the eastern arm which has been rebuilt. This view shows the cross on the high altar and the interior of the baldacchino, a post-war addition in the style of Wren. The eastern saucer domes, richly decorated with fine mosaics, contrast sharply with the plain ones at the western end.

Right: A less familiar view of St Paul's Cathedral, from the north.

St Paul's, London

Seldom has any cathedral been so completely dominated by its architect as St Paul's was by Sir Christopher Wren. He designed it after the Great Fire of London in 1666, which had destroyed its Norman and Gothic predecessor, and he lived long enough to see it finished in 1710, supervising the works frequently in person throughout the period. While the great dome was being erected, he would have himself hoisted up in a basket on a rope. In 1723 he was the first person to be buried in the cathedral, under a simple slab of black marble in the crypt, with an exhortation inscribed above on the wall, which reads: '*Lector, si monumentum requiris, circumspice*' ('Reader, if you seek his monument, look around you').

St Paul's had been the seat of a bishop since the 7th century, and the Norman and Gothic cathedral that was raised on the site in the 11th to 13th centuries had been a worthy building for England's capital. Wren, given the chance (as he hoped) to start from scratch and build an entirely new structure for the London of the 17th century with its dominating role in the European scene, produced two designs, but they were rejected by the authorities who still harked back to the Gothic. At the third attempt, he was more successful, by dint of a vaguer scheme which allowed him to make variations. This enabled him to build the splendid mix of classical and Baroque that we see today, without the authorities appreciating it until it was virtually too late. His structure was based on the Latin-cross plan with a dome over the central crossing. It is symmetrical throughout and owes a lot to St Peter's in Rome, although Wren had never visited that great city before working on St Paul's. Work began on the choir and the lovely east end in 1675, the transepts with their fine curved porches followed, and the nave with its remarkable western vestibule next. The western front is in Renaissance style, in two tiers, with Wren's conception of Baroque for the towers.

The greatest architectural achievement, however, was the dome, 31 metres (102 feet) in diameter on a colossal drum supported by the columns of the central crossing below. This dome is not entirely what it may seem: there are in fact three domes, the first, visible inside and gloriously decorated, has behind it a brick cone that supports the lantern on top, and outside the cone is the timber dome sheathed in lead. The total weight of these structures is said to be 69,000 tonnes (68,000 UK tons). The top of the gold cross on the lantern is 111 metres (365 feet) from the ground. Below the dome inside is an architectural curiosity, the Whispering Gallery, whose acoustics allow a person to whisper at one point along the wall and be heard with absolute clarity by another person on the

other side, more than 30 metres (100 feet) away, as if he or she were standing nearby.

The cathedral is decorated with classical and Baroque motifs, sculptured pediments, flat Corinthian-style pilasters, carved and sculptured wood including the beautiful choir stalls by Grinling Gibbons, and wrought-iron grilles and gates by Jean Tijou, the Huguenot French ironsmith who introduced a new era of wrought-ironsmithing into England at the start of the 18th century.

St Paul's has monuments to many British fighting heroes. Nelson and Wellington are buried in the crypt in magnificent tombs, and Kitchener, who had been drowned at sea during the First World War, has a fine recumbent statue below a special memorial in All Souls' Chapel at the western end.

St David's

St David's is the biggest church in Wales. This seems appropriate for the cathedral of the patron saint of Wales, St David, who had set up one of the first churches in Wales on the present site in about A.D. 550. The Vikings destroyed whatever building was there in the 1070s, and in 1180 the present structure was started by Peter de Leia, a Norman cleric who was Bishop of St Davids from 1176 to 1198. He was responsible for the first nave, distinctive for its Norman-style rounded arches. The choir and transepts followed soon afterwards, and in the early 13th century a central tower was built over the crossing. But in 1220 the tower collapsed, causing major damage to both choir and transepts. This may have been the result of earth tremors which have from time to time shaken the district. By the 1250s, however,

Wales's principal cathedral, St David's, in Romanesque and Gothic, nestles in a lovely setting behind a bank of daffodils, the Welsh national flower.

the damaged parts had been rebuilt (except for the tower) much as they are today, and by 1350 the chapel of St Thomas of Canterbury, the east ambulatory and the Lady Chapel had been added. Henry Gower, who was bishop from 1328 to 1347, heightened the nave and chancel, inserted Decorated-style windows and raised the central tower one extra storey. The tower was completed to its present height of 38 metres (125 feet) in the early 16th century.

One of the many interesting features of St David's is the very flat-pitched roof of the nave, made of Irish oak in the last decades of the 15th century. This ceiling has arches of slight fretlike design that look as though they support the roof but in reality hang from it. The original pitch of the roof can be seen from a triangle of stone fragments and mortar on the western side of the central tower.

St David's was built on wet ground that was not properly drained. As a result the floor of the main part slopes significantly, and some of the nave pillars have what may seem a hazardous list. This distortion may have been 'assisted' by periodic earth tremors.

During modern restorations, some bones were found which are

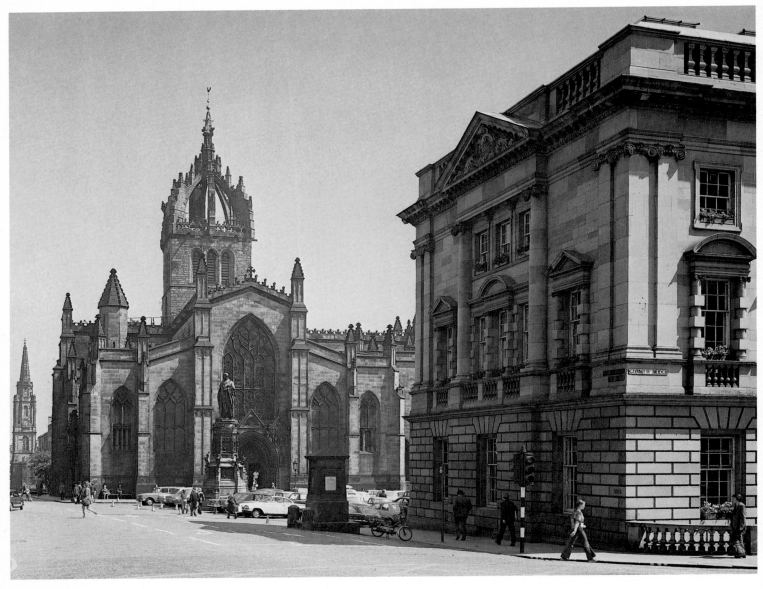

Above: The late Gothic cathedral of St Giles in Edinburgh. The central tower over the crossing is topped by a lantern supported by flying buttresses. It was in St Giles' that rioting broke out in 1637 when Charles I tried to impose a new service book upon the Scottish Church. A parishioner, Jenny Geddes, started it by throwing her stool at the dean.

Right: Looking towards the unusual east end of the Gothic cathedral of St Patrick in Dublin. The cathedral was begun in the 1190s and the main work was done throughout the 13th century.

confidently attributed to the founder himself, and they are interred in a casket of iron and oak in a niche in the western wall of Holy Trinity Chapel to the east of the presbytery. In the centre of the presbytery is the grave of Edmund Tudor, father of Henry VII, the first Welsh king of England and Wales.

Salisbury

Immortalized by the great landscape painter Constable, Salisbury, with its 123-metre (404-foot)-tall spire – the highest in the country – is probably the most swiftly recognizable of all British cathedrals. It is the only English cathedral built in one operation, it has the largest cathedral close, and it is one of the few British cathedrals that was raised on completely virgin ground.

The beginnings of Salisbury stem from a major row between the clergy of an earlier, smaller

cathedral two miles (three kilometres) away at Old Sarum and the military residents of the Norman castle that occupied part of the cathedral ground. Bishop Poore decided to move the entire cathedral set-up, and in 1220 laid the foundations of a brand new structure in the Avon valley beside the village of Milford. The cathedral was to be built in Early English Gothic style, but at the time it is not likely that anyone imagined it would be finished so quickly, in a little over 60 years (except for the central tower and spire). The earliest building was the Trinity Chapel at the extreme east end and this was consecrated in 1225.

Within 33 years the nave with its aisles, two sets of transepts, and the choir had been finished. The building material was chiefly a local cream-shaded stone quarried at Chilmark, with contrasting black and other dark-

coloured marble for some of the piers and columns. Between 1258 and 1266 the western façade was constructed, with its two end towers rising through five diminishing stages to pyramidal tops, the whole faced with niches and blind arcades filled with decorative sculpture. Cloisters were built along the south of the nave, and an interesting octagonal vaulted chapter house on the eastern side of the cloisters, reached by a short passage. This chapter house has geometrical tracery and a fan-vaulted roof supported on a central slim cluster of cylindrical shafts.

In the early part of the 14th century the cathedral was complete but for the central tower. Work began on this feature in the 1330s and it took 50 years or so to build. By the time it was finished the whole cathedral had a unity of design similar to the cathedrals of the Ile de France,

especially Amiens which was also raised in one operation, in about 1220–88. The tower and spire of Salisbury were not raised without difficulty. The piers of the tower were only about 2 metres (6 feet) square, and by no means robust enough to take the weight, thought to be over 6500 tonnes (6400 UK tons), and emergency bolstering had to be introduced in the form of external flying buttresses and other internal support, including the insertion of a pair of reversed strainer arches where the choir transepts meet the central crossing. Even then, further reinforcement was needed in the 15th century. Yet it was all overwhelmingly worthwhile.

Winchester

Winchester was the capital of Anglo-Saxon England, with a senior bishopric and a cathedral. Soon after the Conquest, William of Normandy, intending to retain

Looking down past the choir to the nave and the west end of Salisbury Cathedral, an almost perfect English Gothic church interior.

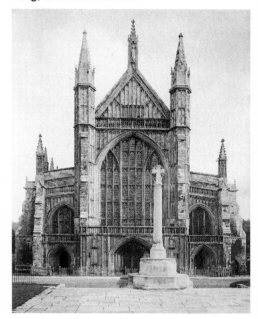

Winchester as his capital, instructed Bishop Walkelyn to begin a new Norman cathedral, and between 1079 and 1093 the two transepts were built of limestone brought to the site from quarries on the Isle of Wight. These are the oldest and most complete parts of the cathedral, and are unusual for having their one-storey aisles running round the transept ends. The aisle, triforium and clerestory arches are rounded, springing out of cylindrical columns with undecorated cushion capitals. The round-headed windows are deeply recessed. At the same time, or shortly afterwards, the Norman nave of 12 bays was built on clustered columns. A central tower was raised over the crossing, but this collapsed in 1107 and was not replaced until

the next century. In the 13th century work started on the retrochoir and the Lady Chapel in the eastern arm, which was finished in the 14th century.

The major work at Winchester, however, which transformed the cathedral into the remarkable horizontal Gothic building, 169 metres (556 feet) in length and the longest Gothic church in Europe, was carried out in a tremendous double spurt of activity in the 14th century, first under Bishop Edington (1346–66) and then by the great William of Wykeham, bishop from 1366 to 1404, who was also twice Lord Chancellor of England. William of Wykeham funded the greater part of his works out of his own pocket, and employed William Wynford as chief designer-mason. His principal achievement was the

transformation of the nave. The Norman nave had been three-storeyed, with triforium and clerestory, all with round-headed arches on tall, slender columns. The height was retained but the Norman work was ingeniously encased in Perpendicular-style stonework, with much taller and pointed main arcade arches, with balcony fronted by a parapet on a frieze of corbels, and above that a clerestory of recessed windows. The roof was altered into a wonderful network of Perpendicular lierne vaulting whose ribs spring from the tops of the altered Norman piers at a point a third of the way up the clerestory, giving an impression of a low nave. This is balanced, however, by the tremendously long vista from the west end right into the central crossing.

Winchester has some fine 13th-century ceiling and wall paintings, a 12th-century font of black marble from Tournai, at which Henry III was baptized as a baby in 1207, and a set of 60 fine misericords in the beautiful choir stalls of the 1320s. The cathedral projects over the foundations of the old Saxon cathedral in which several kings were buried, the most famous of whom was Canute who, though not an Anglo-Saxon, came to love the English and ruled them well. His bones are now in a mortuary chest in the choir, alongside those of other early rulers including William II (Rufus) who was killed by an arrow during a hunt in the New Forest in 1100.

York Minster

York Minster gets more visitors than any cathedral or abbey in Britain except Westminster and St Paul's. Not surprisingly, for it is really a marvellous monument to medieval building skills. And of course its superb position in the high part of York, enabling it to tower above almost everything else, makes it a natural draw to the millions who come to this ancient walled city every year, giving them an unforgettable climax to their enjoyment. Leaving aside the city's Roman origins, its ecclesiastical history is one of England's longest. The archbishopric was founded in 732 but York had been a bishopric since 627 when Paulinus baptized King Edwin of Northumbria on the site. Edwin ordered a stone church to be built immediately afterwards. This was burned down and then rebuilt, but the massive structure we see today is very largely the work of the long period from about 1220 to 1474. Basically Gothic in its successive English manifestations, Early English, Decorated and Perpendicular, York is the largest medieval cathedral in England, with the greatest amount of surviving medieval stained glass.

The cathedral was built on cruciform plan, with transepts 68 metres (223 feet) wide and nave with aisle each side 81 metres (265 feet) long, reaching 29 metres (95 feet) to a wooden ceiling, a height only exceeded in England at Westminster. The north transept is dominated by a magnificent window of five equal lancets at its north end, almost filling the whole wall, which is known as the 'Five Sisters' and was finished in about 1250. The east end of the cathedral, containing the choir, high altar and Lady Chapel, dates largely from the mid-14th century and is actually longer than the nave. Its crowning feature is the great East Window which, like a wall of glass, fills practically the whole east end. It is 23 metres (76 feet) tall and 10 metres (32 feet) wide. The choir, with its stone choir screen, dates from the 15th century, though the wonderful choir stalls of carved wood were destroyed in a fire started by a lunatic in 1829, and have been replaced in Gothic style.

The 14th-century western front at York is striking. It has three portals, somewhat dwarfed by the proud buttresses between and the huge, rich traceried west window (which was glazed in the 1330s) whose base sits as it were upon the centre portal. The front is flanked by two towers, the south built between 1433 and 1447, and the north between 1465 and 1474. Topped with fine pinnacles, they are 60 metres (196 feet) tall, the north tower housing Great Peter, an 11-tonne (10¾-ton) bell. Over the central crossing is the cathedral's third tower, a splendid creation of the early 15th century, 20 metres (65 feet) square and rising to about 55 metres (180 feet), with a stone vault.

One of the more unusual features of York is its octagonal chapter house, of the 1340s, added to the north-east corner of the north transept and connected by a right-angled vestibule. It is lit by seven traceried windows of five lights each, containing much original glass.

Above: The largest medieval cathedral in England, York Minster, from the south-west, an ideal setting when seen from beside the medieval city wall.

Right: Some of the stained glass in the Jesse Window at York Minster dates from the early 14th century. Depicted on the central lancet here are Christ and the Virgin Mary.

Left: The face of Christ, a detail from the 13th-century wall paintings in the Chapel of the Holy Sepulchre at Winchester Cathedral.

Cathedrals of France

Albi

Many cathedrals and churches have features that seem more appropriate to castles – towers with narrow windows, arrow loops, battlements, tall transepts fortified with pilaster buttresses (like Cefalù), and gatehouses with heavy portcullises protecting approach to the precincts. But the massive, purple-brick cathedral of St Cécile at Albi, some 50 miles (80 kilometres) north-east of

Looking down upon the 16th-century screen at Albi Cathedral, whose exquisite carving is heightened by the natural lighting of the interior.

Toulouse in the historic district of Languedoc, was purposely designed and constructed as a fortress cathedral. Founded in the 1270s by the fierce and brutal bishop Bertrand de Castanet, who was Grand Inquisitor following the ruthless suppression of the Albigensian heretics in southern France in the 13th century (200 were said to have been burned alive on one day in 1244), Albi Cathedral looks more like a Castilian castle than a medieval church.

Raised as a rectangular hall about 30 metres (100 feet) high and nearly 18 metres (60 feet) wide, with its east end polygonal in plan and its west end crowned with a 91-metre (300-foot) castlelike tower, Albi's exterior is surrounded by semicylindrical buttresses interspersed with pilaster projections containing enormously tall and narrow round-headed windows. Around the top of the hall parapet are machicolations. The cylindrical buttress-turrets clasping the corners of the tower are pierced only by arrow loops. There are no entrances at the west end; the main entrance, on its south side, is protected by a richly carved stone porch, added in the late 15th century and the only ornamented feature on the exterior. The walls are up to 5 metres (15 feet) thick, and though built of brick, presented a formidable obstacle to attackers.

Inside, Albi is aisleless and without transepts. It is spacious and well proportioned. There are chapels at two levels all round the hall, between the buttresses (which project prominently inwards) and within the thickness of the walls, a feature of Barcelona Cathedral whose design was influenced by that of Albi. The choir screen, of about 1500, is a masterpiece of carving.

Albi was built between about

1275 and 1500, the greater part of the work being finished before 1400. The cathedral was besieged several times. Today, a fine view of its impregnable appearance on the left bank of the Tarn can be obtained from La Madeleine, the district on the other side of the river.

Amiens

This marvellous Gothic achievement, whose main structure was completed inside 70 years (1220–88), is the last of the Ile de France Gothic cathedrals of the 13th century. Covering 7800 square metres (84,000 square feet), it is also the biggest cathedral in France, large enough in its first years to accommodate the entire population of Amiens, about 10,000 people. The length is 134 metres (438 feet) and the height of the nave an astounding 43 metres (140 feet). Its short building time has given it a unity of design, like its contemporary Salisbury. And yet there were flaws in Amiens. Within a century of completion, major repairs were having to be carried out; the

The exterior of Albi epitomizes the concept of the fortress-cathedral. It has an impregnable look. Even the gate at the left would be more appropriate on a castle wall.

These stone figures, representing the Annunciation, the Visitation and the Presentation, are among the remarkable stone sculpture surviving in Amiens Cathedral from the early 13th century.

north tower required reinforcement, the north aisle of the choir had to be strengthened with additional piers, and tie rods had to be inserted into the triforium passage. It was as well, for the repairs enabled the cathedral to last into this century for us to enjoy.

The cathedral was built upon the site of three earlier succeeding churches, the last having been gutted by fire in 1218. The foundation stone of the new work was laid by the bishop, Evrard de Fouilloy, in 1220 and the design was the brainchild of master mason Robert de Luzarches, who actually inscribed his name in the nave. Unusually for cathedral-builders, he started with the nave and west front, completing the

former and reaching as far as the bases of the top storeys of the west towers by 1236. The choir was not started until 1239, but within 30 years it was completed, along with its lovely ambulatory and apsidal chapels, and the transepts. Side chapels were added in the 14th century.

The west front has been described as disappointing, but it is a noble sight with its three dramatic deeply recessed portals whose points rise between prominent buttresses, and with the exquisite figure sculpture in the recesses. Above are two galleries, the topmost spanned by arched niches filled with more statuary. Admittedly this higher gallery obscures some of the bottom of the glorious traceried

rose window (added in the 15th century), but it is arguable whether this is in fact a particularly serious design fault.

Bourges
St Etienne's Gothic cathedral is the seat of the archbishop of Bourges, and it stands at the top of the city, some 125 miles (200 kilometres) south of Paris. Built chiefly in the 13th century and homogeneous in its structure, its style deriving to a great extent from the Ile de France cathedrals, it is distinguished externally by its long, slim, rectangular shape, with flying buttresses along both sides and round the bold eastern apsidal end, which reach up and over the lower and higher aisle roofs into the continuous nave,

choir and chancel clerestory walls. The west front is different from those of the Ile de France cathedrals in having five, not three, portals, in Bourges's case all topped by tall triangular arches. The two flanking towers are different. Built in the 14th century, the north tower collapsed in 1506 and was rebuilt with less than faithful adherence to the original. The five portals are richly decorated with sculpture both in the tympana over the doorways and the surrounding polylobes, though the niches in the vertical splays between the doorways suffered terribly from the vandalism endured by the cathedral in both the 16th and the 18th centuries. Above the central portal is a fine centrepiece of two

The western façade of Amiens Cathedral is rendered less than perfect by the inequality of the towers, but withal it is a noble front.

tall, beautifully traceried windows side by side, over which is an unusual wheel window. Leading up to the front is an impressive flight of steps stretching from end to end.

It is the interior of Bourges that commands such respect and wonder. Described as one of the most remarkable ever built, unique for the combination of breadth and height, it enables the visitor to understand almost at a glance from any vantage point what Gothic architecture is all about. The plan is a long and wide nave leading directly in line to a choir and then an apsidal chancel, outside of which are two aisles each side continuing also in line to a double ambulatory at the eastern end. It has no transepts. The outer aisles rise to about 9 metres (30 feet), with windows, and in the 15th to 16th centuries had the spaces between their buttresses filled with chapels the entire length of both sides. The inner aisles rise to 21 metres (69 feet), with a clerestory of pairs or triples of lancet windows. In the centre the nave rises to 38 metres (125 feet), its immensely tall and slender shafted columns carrying

its side arches clear of the inner-aisle clerestory and supporting a second clerestory of its own, with lancet windows topped by medallion windows for each bay. This provides a splendid flood of light such as is not found in any of the other major Gothic cathedrals.

Bourges has a vast crypt, the east end of which was built with great technical skill to cater for the sloping ground below, in which ran the old city moat, the crypt acting as a base for the four-storey apsidal end above. It has the tomb of Jean, duc de Berri (1340–1416), third son of John II of France and one of the cathedral's great benefactors, who financed the major work on the west front and also much of the glorious stained glass of Bourges which in some quarters is compared with that of Chartres.

The cathedral was vandalized by Huguenots during the mid-16th-century wars of religion and for a time it was even in danger of being demolished. During the French Revolution it suffered further desecration, when many of its furnishings and works of art were destroyed.

Below: Bourges Cathedral has no transepts, and its whole astonishing interior can be grasped at one time.

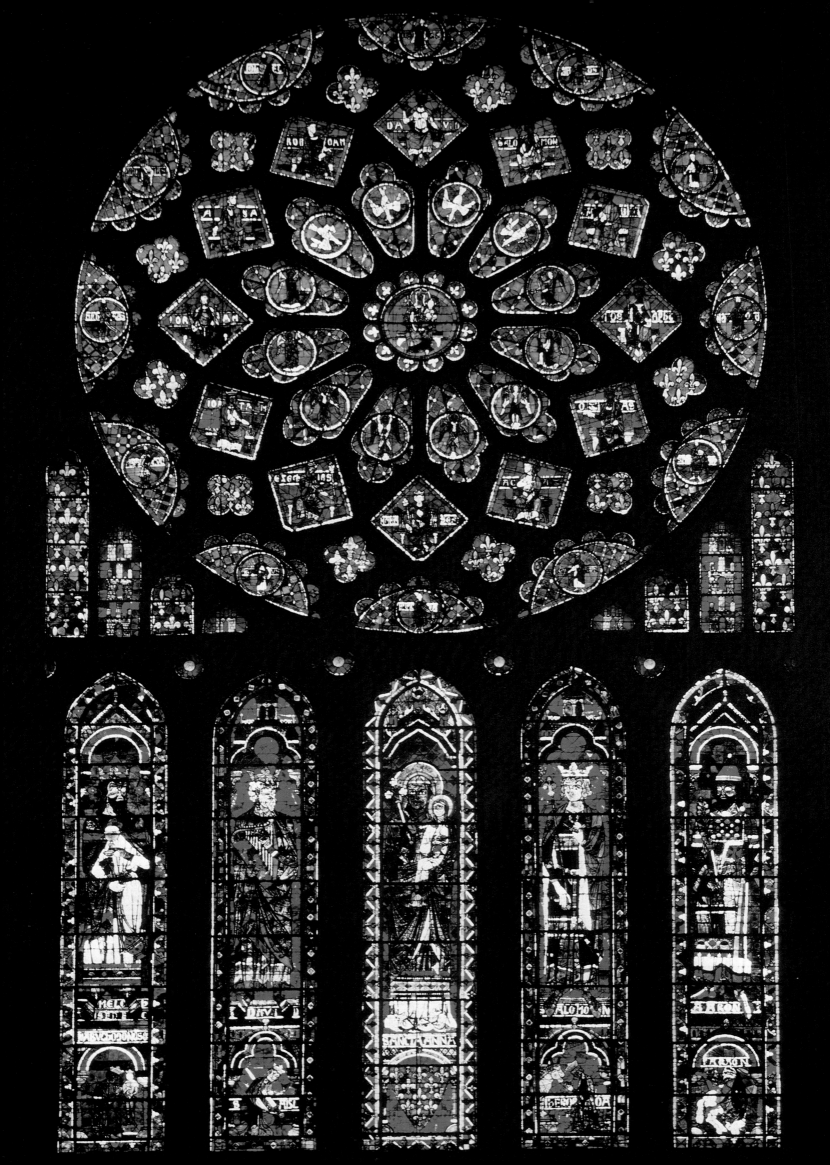

Chartres

Here is a cathedral about which everyone goes into raptures. Pure Gothic in style, adorned with an astonishing amount of the finest stone sculpture, and glazed with a profusion of the most beautiful stained glass ever made, which led medieval visitors to describe it as jewellery, Chartres is certainly a building to wonder at. Fortunately for posterity some of the original intentions of the architects were not carried out. For example, it was once to have had eight steeples, but has ended up with only two, these different, not matching, which allow us to appreciate all its other exterior features without intrusion.

Chartres is cruciform in plan with a long nave like the other cathedrals in the Ile de France, which heralded the Gothic style in architecture in Europe in the 12th century. The nave, 130 metres (427 feet) long, is over 35 metres (120 feet) tall and its high vaults are supported by flying buttresses, the first flying buttresses to be built as an integral part of a cathedral structure. Its east end, also supported with flying buttresses, has radiating chapels leading off the ambulatory surrounding the choir. From the west end you can see clearly and without interruption right to the easternmost rounded apse, the view enhanced by the slender shafted piers through the triforium to the glorious Gothic windows with their stained glass of the 12th and 13th centuries. This resplendent decorative glass tells a succession of stories from the New Testament. The apogee of the treatment is to be found in the three rose windows in west, south and north fronts.

The west façade of Chartres contains the Portail Royal (Royal Portal), constructed in the mid-12th century and less dramatic than those of other Ile de France cathedrals. It has three portals profusely decorated with sculptured figures of Christ, saints and biblical details, notably in the tympana of all three. Above is a

37

Above: The central stages of the western façade of Chartres Cathedral balance superbly with the asymmetrical towers and tall steeples, giving an exciting anticipation of the cathedral's interior.

Above right: Two of the earliest Gothic cathedral towers in Europe, gloriously decorated with pierced parapets and bold, sure-footed oxen leaning through the arcades, crown the western façade of Laon Cathedral.

second tier of recessed lancets beneath the triumphant centrepiece of the whole façade, the west rose window whose coloured glass is devoted to the Last Judgement. Flanking this façade are the two towers with their spires, the south (1140s) beginning square and changing to octagonal where the graceful pyramidal spire begins its upward thrust to a 106-metre (349-foot) point, the north tower (of 1134), also square but rising in more flamboyant style into a narrower but more elaborate spire of 115 metres (377 feet) built as late as the 16th century.

Chartres was started in the 1130s on the site of an earlier cathedral. A disastrous fire in 1194 destroyed a great part of the work, but within 70-odd years – not a lot of time by medieval cathedral-building standards – the whole cathedral was completed, except for the north spire and some work on the transepts, in time for its dedication by King Louis IX in 1260. Thereafter, it was the rest of the sculpture and glazing that had to be finished, and what a marvellous flood of colour and imagery emerged!

Laon

At the top of a steep hill in the city of Laon, capital of the province of Aisne, stands the first complete Gothic cathedral built in France. Begun in about 1160, the great bulk of the work was finished by about 1230, and has been altered but little since. To a greater or lesser extent it served as a model for many others that followed, such as Chartres, Notre-Dame (Paris) and Reims, perhaps most notably in its new concept of west front with recessed portals, rose window and tall western towers.

There had been a church at Laon in the late 11th century. It was badly damaged in 1113 when an angry mob set it on fire as the result of some aggravation on the part of the then bishop. Then, in about 1160, Bishop Gauthier de Montagne initiated a new two-phase building programme, which embraced some 70 years.

The first phase, from 1160 to 1180, saw the construction of the sanctuary with its square apse, and the first bays of the transepts. The second phase, lasting longer, was also much more productive. The transepts were finished, the four-storeyed nave based on slim, cylindrical piers was built, the choir was added and the west front was erected. This west front has three portals, with deeply recessed porches, the centre one slightly taller than the outer two, with some very finely sculptured figures in the voussoirs and tympana. The rose window gives the impression of a wheel in rotation. The two towers are square with polygonal corners, open with pierced parapets at the top, surmounting carved stone oxen standing between slender arcading on the corners. These towers are repeated in the same style over the transepts. The central crossing is topped by a lantern with a pyramidal roof. At the outer end of each transept is a polygonal apsed chapel, with handsome outside buttresses drawing your eyes to the conical roof.

The interior of Laon was circuited by the triforium that was hollowed out of the walls, and linked to spiral staircases in the towers and to a remarkable arrangement of spirals within the four main crossing piers leading to the gallery around the lantern. The four storeys contain a happy mix of round-headed and pointed arches.

Laon was once lit by over 2000 stained-glass windows, but only a handful of these remain today, notably the rose window on the north transept which represents the seven liberal arts of St Augustine. The ample window area lights up the interior even on a dull day.

Notre-Dame, Paris

The Cathedral of Notre-Dame enjoys the advantage of standing upon an island site in the Seine as it runs through the centre of France's capital city. This enables one to see the cathedral in its full glory from any of the four flanks (though there is obstruction upon the north-west side). And what a splendid choice of views the visitor gets: from the west, the superbly proportioned five-stage western façade; from the south, the incredible south transept façade whose top half is almost entirely filled with glass; and from the east, the rounded apsidal end

with its radiating flying buttresses in rounded-arch form continuing round and along the sides of the chancel, looking, as one architectural historian commented, like the oars of a Roman galley.

Notre-Dame is one of the earliest and most typical Gothic cathedrals, those marvellous buildings that set the new Gothic style firmly into the mainstream of European architectural history. It was started in 1163 to replace a smaller Romanesque cathedral on the site, under the vigorous direction of the bishop of Paris, Maurice de Sully, who had started life as a humble wood-gatherer's son, and continued with equally enthusiastic encouragement by Philip Augustus, king of France from 1180 to 1223. Cruciform in plan, it was to have a long, tall nave flanked with double aisles, chapels along the walls and between buttresses, moderately projecting but lofty transepts, and an apsidal eastern arm. In this arm is a fine

The interior of Laon Cathedral has harmonious flights of one-, two- and three-arched storeys rising to the light-giving clerestories.

39

chancel which in the late 13th and early 14th centuries was complemented by the addition of a triple chapel at the chancel head and other chapels on both sides.

The western façade of Notre-Dame was begun at the end of the 12th century and by the 1250s had all the features which were to make it one of the most swiftly recognizable of all the Gothic cathedral façades. The first (ground) stage was the row of three huge recessed portals, sculpture-filled right across. Over this was built a gallery of niches with statuary, spanning the width, and this was surmounted by a

stage containing the rose window of wheel design between rectangular stages of the flanking towers. Above these was raised an arcade of interlaced arches on tall, very slim columns, topped by a shallow breakfront balustrade behind which rise the top stages of the square towers, the north one slightly broader than the south.

Inside the cathedral one is perhaps disappointed by the sombre darkness which is met within the aisles, despite the high nave – over 30 metres (100 feet) – which is supported on lofty shafts down to the capitals of 6·5-metre

Above: The cathedral of Notre-Dame is one of the greatest buildings in Paris, a supreme Gothic achievement.

Right: The western façade at Reims Cathedral was once a mass of exquisite figurative sculpture, brutally damaged by both civilian and foreign assault, and it is today being restored with unmatched skill and care.

(21-foot) cylindrical piers from which spring the pointed arches holding the gallery and the clerestory above. This is because the addition of sloping roofs over the aisles, a later work when the nave was heightened and big windows put in the clerestory, reduced the illumination possible from the aisles. Some compensation was achieved by enlarging the transept window area by converting the walls into virtual window frames and putting into the gable end two circular windows, one, 6 metres (19 feet) across, over the other, which is 12 metres (40 feet) across and is almost the width of the transept itself.

Notre-Dame was badly damaged inside and on the exterior by revolutionaries in the 1790s, and much restoration was done by Viollet-le-Duc in the mid-19th century.

Reims

This is the coronation cathedral of the French kings. Joan of Arc, who promised to lead the troops of Charles VII to victory against the English, drive them out of their possessions and put the crown of France upon Charles's head, fulfilled her mission and witnessed here the anointing of the king in 1429. By then, Reims, one of the early French Gothic masterpieces, was already complete – but only just. The top storeys of its two west towers had been finished in 1427. As the king walked towards the western doors he would have been overwhelmed, no doubt, by the profusion of sculpture that filled (and still fills) almost every niche and space upon the great façade, whose central motif is the rose window.

Gothic Reims was begun in 1211, following the destruction by fire a decade before of a very early church on the site, founded in the Dark Ages. In this earlier church, Clovis, king of the Franks, had been anointed and this established Reims as France's coronation church. The choir of the new cathedral, with its radiating chapels, the superb flying buttresses of the eastern apse that rise out of the inwards curves of the chapels, and the transepts with their stained-glass windows

were all ready by 1241. Work then began on the nave and western façade, and by 1285 the nave was complete. This was followed by a long period of sporadic work, and even when the 14th century turned into the 15th, Reims still lacked the top stages of its western towers. But when it was all done, it was probably the most magnificent cathedral then standing in France. Almost 139 metres (454 feet) long inside, the nave rising to 38 metres (125 feet), it was consistently uniform in style because each architect followed the patterns of his predecessor.

The real glory of Reims lies in its sculpture, most particularly the figures and the vegetation motifs. The inside of the west front, for example, is dominated by a trelliswork of niches with figures, set in tiers separated by panels of

intricate and natural foliage. The three portals on the western façade are lavishly decorated with some of the most vivid stone portraiture in France, and there are many hundreds of figures. Each has an expression of its own, individual and meaningful, like the angel in the Annunciation tableau in the central portal, who is smiling.

Reims has suffered terrible damage in the last four centuries – ravages by Protestant iconoclasts, vandalism by Revolutionaries in the 1790s, and as many as 300 direct hits by shells and bombs from German forces in the First World War – but it has also been enjoying a long period of creative restoration by French craftsmen, at least matching the superb regenerative work done on the west façade at Wells Cathedral in England.

Cathedrals of Belgium and Holland

Belgium

St Michael's, Brussels

The cathedral of St Michael stands on a hill overlooking the Belgian capital's centre, near the lovely Parc de Bruxelles. It is the national church of Belgium, Gothic in style, with a western façade that reminds one of that at Westminster Abbey. This façade is floodlit in summer to show to the highest advantage the colouring of the glass and masonry of the great west windows.

St Michael's was built over more than three centuries, beginning in 1226 upon the remains of an earlier church in Romanesque style. This earlier church witnessed the ceremonial burial beneath it of the remains of St Gudule, a saintly woman of the 7th century who performed miracles in the Brussels district. The present cathedral contains some of the earliest Gothic work in Belgium, though not much remains of the first buildings. What has survived is part of the choir, begun in 1226, which has a fine apsidal end and is flanked by two large side chapels whose windows were later glazed with some of the best stained glass in Belgium, by Bernard van Orley (1492–1542), the Flemish painter patronized by Margaret of Austria (regent of the Netherlands 1507–

Right: The huge tower of Malines (Mechelen) Cathedral was once meant to rise to nearly 170 metres (550 feet), but its present soaring 97 metres (319 feet) is in fine proportion to the remainder of the structure.

Below: Modern buildings cannot dwarf or detract from the dominating height and magnificence of St Michael and St Gudule's Gothic cathedral in Brussels, whose west front has an almost perfect symmetry.

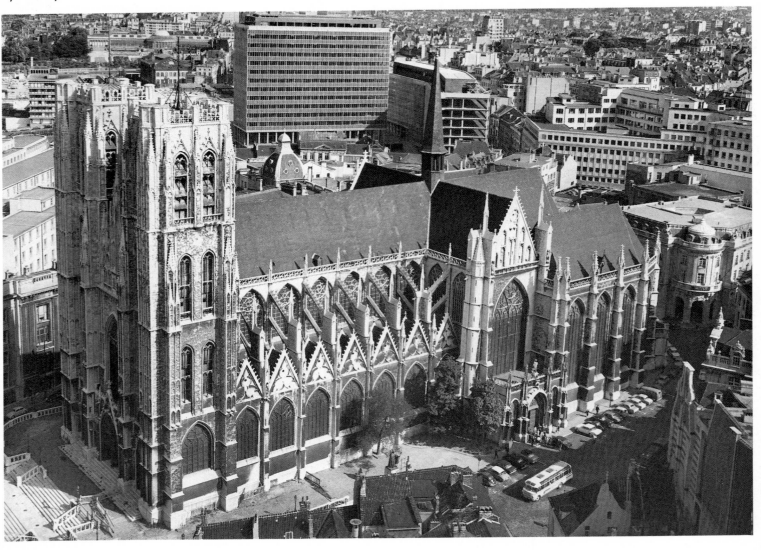

30), who was born in, and held court at, Brussels. Beneath the choir are buried several dukes of Brabant.

In the 15th century the great nave was constructed, whose cylindrical columns were later adorned with beautifully sculptured statues of the apostles standing on ornate corbels, a motif repeated at Malines and intended to symbolize the idea that the columns supported the vault of which Christ was the crown. The west façade had been begun in the 13th century, but it was not until the early 16th that Jan van Ruysbroeck's two towers were added, rising to 69 metres (226 feet). At this height, however, they were stopped and have never been completed. Some of the stained glass in the façade is by Cornelis de Vriendt (also known as Cornelis Floris).

St Michael's was the church of the Order of the Golden Fleece, where its principal ceremonies were held. This was the highest honour the Burgundian Court could bestow.

Malines

Malines, which is called Mechelen in Flemish, is in the province of Antwerp. The archbishop of Malines is also the primate of all Belgium, an office established in 1559. The cathedral is dedicated to St Rombout, an Irish monk of the 8th century who founded an abbey at Malines and who was later martyred.

St Rombout's was begun in 1217 after drainage of some of the marshy ground between the two tributaries of the river Dijle that runs through the city. The lower parts of the nave and the transepts were the first works. In the 1340s the choir was started, in Gothic style, with a fine ambulatory. The choir was adorned, much later, with a remarkable Baroque altar by Fayd'herbe, a pupil of Rubens. In the 14th century, the nave was finished, its triforium being supported through cylindrical columns with polygonal capitals, and in the 17th and 18th century statues of the apostles were applied on corbels on the columns, as at St Michael's in Brussels.

The interior of the cathedral is filled with distinguished works of art, several by Michiel Coxie who was born at Malines in 1499, including his *San Sebastian*. In the south transept there is an altarpiece of about 1627 depicting the Crucifixion by Van Dyck, and there are also paintings of the story of St Rombout in both transepts.

The dominant feature of the cathedral, however, is its single, lofty western tower. This was designed by Wauthier Coolmans in the mid-15th century and built between 1452 and 1578. The original plans have survived, showing what it would have looked like if it had been finished. It would have risen to 167 metres (548 feet) had its spire been built. As it is, though the scheme was abandoned after the tower had reached its present height of 97 metres (319 feet), it is still a remarkable tower, up to the top of which there are 558 steps. The foundations on which it rests are less than 3 metres (9 feet) thick. The tower contains Belgium's finest carillon, of 49 bells, many of which date from the 15th and 16th centuries. Vauban, the celebrated French military engineer who served Louis XIV from 1655 to 1703, once described the tower as the Eighth Wonder of the World.

During the First World War, Malines was in the front line of battle, and was several times bombarded by the Germans. The archbishop, Cardinal Mercier, encouraged the citizens not to give in, issuing his famous pastoral letter 'Patriotism and Endurance'. After he died in 1926 he was buried there. The cathedral has been restored since the Second World War.

Tournai

The greatest cathedral of Belgium, Notre-Dame at Tournai is arrestingly impressive in its Romanesque and Gothic styles, which are clearly separated from one another on the exterior elevation. The cathedral has five tall towers – all of the same height, some 82 metres (270 feet) – four of them capped with single pyramidal spires. It has semicylindrically apsed transepts which are remarkable structures in themselves, with aisles and triforium, and its dark exterior colouring comes from the black marble used as one of its building materials.

There was a Roman outpost at Tournai. Childeric I, king of the Franks, who died in 481, had his capital there. His son, Clovis, became a Christian in 496, and he may have built a church on the site, that was converted later into a Carolingian basilica church in the 800s. The later church was sacked by Vikings sailing up the Scheldt, in 881. Then, in the late 11th century, Notre-Dame was begun.

The long, four-storeyed Romanesque nave, with columns graced with fine capitals, flanked on both sides by aisles of lower height, was built between 1110 and 1150. In 1146, Tournai became a bishopric, and the cathedral was consecrated about 30 years later. In the 1150s, work began on one of its most unusual features, the apsed and aisled transepts which reveal Gothic influence said to have come from masons who had worked on Ile de France cathedrals, and which were decorated with frescoes. Above the transepts the five towers were raised during the period 1150 to 1250, the central tower being topped later with a lantern. The other four clasp the transepts in pairs at the point where the apses begin.

Some time in the 1240s, a new Gothic choir replaced the earlier Romanesque one, and it was built by Bishop Walter de Marvis, employing French masons who are believed to have been working at Soissons. The western façade has been remodelled more than once, but it still retains many examples of early 14th-century sculpture executed by the local

The five towers of Tournai Cathedral in Belgium are late Romanesque, each of them 82 metres (270 feet) tall.

school of sculptors that was developing at Tournai.

By about 1500, Tournai had reached the size it is today and its windows had been gloriously paned with stained glass, but the pyramidal spires had yet to be added – later in the century. In 1566, in the wake of the Reformation and the wars of religion, Notre-Dame was badly spoliated by Protestant iconoclasts. But in 1570 the distinguished Flemish artist Cornelis de Vriendt (1514–75)

began to work at Tournai and he created the superb rood screen of polychrome marble and presumably superintended restoration of the damage of 1566.

Among the host of treasures at Tournai are an extremely early Byzantine ivory cross of the 6th century, a diptych of St Nicaise, a superb reliquary of the Virgin Mary executed in the 13th century by Nicholas of Verdun, in gold and enamel and studded with precious stones, and a Purgatory by Rubens.

The high altar in front of the fine apsidal east end with its huge radiating lights at Tournai Cathedral.

Holland

's Hertogenbosch

If you could climb upon the flying buttresses of St John's Cathedral at 's Hertogenbosch, you would see, better than you can from the ground, an amazing procession of stone manikins 'scrambling over the buttresses to escape from the demons pursuing them'. This is just one of the more fantastic forms of decoration on the exterior of this ornate 15th-century Brabantine Gothic cathedral, within which Hieronymus Bosch, the Dutch painter who was born at 's Hertogenbosch in 1450, once worked and where the great scholar and humanist, Erasmus, worshipped when a student at school there.

's Hertogenbosch is the capital of the province of North Brabant, and it is near the river Maas. It used to be known as Bois-le-Duc, because of the Flemish duke of Brabant, Henry I, who in the 12th century built a hunting lodge there. It later became a fortress. In the 13th century, when Holland was a collection of small states nominally part of the Holy Roman Empire, a church was begun at 's Hertogenbosch, and it was dedicated to St John (St Jan).

Early in the 15th century the church was radically reshaped in a style of Gothic that differed from the more conventionally plain Dutch form, making it the most dramatic and important 15th-century ecclesiastical building in Holland, and putting it among the greatest of European Gothic cathedrals. Centred upon a towering 34-metre (110-foot)-high nave (carried on 150 pillars), with four side aisles, five transepts, a bold and massive western tower (which incorporates the smaller original 13th-century west tower), and a cupola-topped lantern tower over the crossing, the cathedral represents the apogee of Gothic decoration in Holland. The south façade is superbly ornate, with a double-arched porch.

Inside, the choir has richly carved stalls and there are radiating chapels, and a flamboyantly carved altar frontal of about 1500. The baptismal font at the west end of the south aisle is of bronze and was executed by

The short east end of 's Hertogenbosch Cathedral is overawed by the cupola-topped lantern tower over the central crossing.

Jan Aerts of Maastricht in the 1490s. The Lady Chapel contains a 13th-century statue to the Virgin Mary which is an object of pilgrimage. Perhaps the richest decorative work, in both wood and stone, stems from the 16th century.

's Hertogenbosch Cathedral was formally handed over to the Protestants in 1629, but when Napoleon appropriated Holland and made one of his brothers, Louis, its king, he reassigned the cathedral to the Catholic Church.

Utrecht

Dutch cathedrals are, on the whole, simpler, more austere and less decorated than their neighbours in Belgium, France and Germany. Two exceptions are 's Hertogenbosch and Utrecht. The latter began as a Gothic structure of the mid-13th century upon the site of a much older church, a building started in the late 7th century by a Frankish ruler for St Willibrord (c. 657–c. 738), an English missionary to the Low Countries who became archbishop of the Frisians at the end of the 7th century and who held his ministry at Utrecht.

The Gothic cathedral at Utrecht is dedicated to St Martin, and is built in warm, coloured brick. It became a Protestant cathedral in the 17th century. It is a unique building in that its western end is separated from the rest of the church by an open space, where once the nave had been. The nave had collapsed during a hurricane in 1674 and, curiously, the space has never been filled. The west end consists of a tremendously impressive tower, nearly 104 metres (340 feet) high, built in the 14th century and given a carillon in the 1660s. The tower is said to be a prototype for several other towers in Holland. It was built by the first architect on record as having worked at the cathedral, Jan I van den Dom, otherwise known as Magister Johannes de Hannovia.

The surviving eastern part of the cathedral is chiefly of 14th-century to 16th-century work, and consists of a lofty choir about 35 metres (115 feet) tall, with an apsidal east end and a gallery, whose triforium and clerestory are well-proportioned, two transepts and some fine cloisters on the end of the south transept, beyond which was built a chapter house that is now part of the buildings of Utrecht University. On the whole, the decoration of this eastern end is austere, but the choir has some impressive and elaborate tombs whose carving is of very high quality, notably one early monument to Bishop Guy d'Avesnes (d. 1317). The cathedral is lit from large windows with exquisite tracery. Beneath the choir and the vanished nave is a crypt in which are preserved numerous relics, including the hearts of both Conrad II (Holy Roman Emperor 1024–39) and Henry V (Holy Roman Emperor 1105–25).

The small space between the western tower and the south transept end of Utrecht Cathedral marks the empty space where the original nave once stood.

Cathedrals of Central Europe

Austria

Salzburg

Birthplace of the musical genius Mozart, festival city, and one of the gems of Austria, Salzburg abounds in distinctive, noble buildings. Principal among these is the great cathedral, once described as the most perfect specimen of Renaissance style in the Germanic lands. Though it is in the lower part of the city, about 150 metres (150 yards) from the river Salzach, and under the shadow of the towers of Salzburg's ancient fortress on the hill, the cathedral is still conspicuous, its grandeur enhanced by the open piazzas that bound three of its sides.

The bishopric of Salzburg was created as long ago as about A.D. 700 by the Irish-born St Rupert. Three-quarters of a century later, another Irish bishop, St Virgil, consecrated the first cathedral. In the 10th century, Salzburg was devastated by Magyar raids and only partly rebuilt. Towards the end of the 12th century, renovations began. The cathedral received a fine nave flanked by four aisles (two on each side) and crowned with a lantern tower. More alterations and additions were made in the centuries that followed, but at the beginning of the 17th, much of the cathedral was pulled down to allow a major reconstruction, which is substantially what can be seen today.

At first, it was to be rebuilt to a remarkable scheme of Vincenzo Scamozzi (1552–1616), the great Italian architect, but his plan was never carried out. Instead, another set of designs was commissioned from Santino Solari, and in about 1611 work began. Solari's new cathedral was cruciform on Latin-cross plan and had a great domed basilica with no aisles but with three apses, one at the choir end and the other two on the ends of the north and south transepts. The western façade was two-towered, in Roman Baroque style. Lighting that would normally have been provided if there had been aisles flooded into the interior through the round-headed lights set about the circumference of the drum of the cupola on the lantern. Although the cathedral is tall and narrow, on a sunny day it is brilliantly lit.

The design of Salzburg Cathedral followed closely the ecclesiastical building styles then flourishing in Rome, and at first sight one is instantly reminded of St Peter's. The interior decorative work is superb, with memorable frescoes and much exciting stucco work.

St Stephen's, Vienna

Standing today with other medieval buildings inside the famous enclosure formed by the

Below: The central crossing in the fine Roman Baroque cathedral at Salzburg is superbly illuminated by well-conceived window arrangements.

Right: In the middle of the old city of Salzburg the great green dome of the 17th-century cathedral rises behind the twin towers of the western façade.

Right: Towering over the ancient and romantic city of Vienna are St Stephen's Gothic cathedral (right) and (left) St Peter's Baroque church.

Below: Part of the vast, steep roofing of St Stephen's Cathedral, decorated with patterned tiles. Note the motif of the eagle of the imperial Hapsburgs.

The gloriously carved pulpit at St Stephen's Cathedral, the work of Anton Pilgram.

Ringstrasse and a canal from the Danube, a major reconstruction work carried out by Emperor Franz Josef of Austria in the years 1858–88, St Stephen's (St Stephan's) is still one of the most distinguished buildings in that romantic and beautiful European capital, Vienna. Instantly recognizable from its vast, steep roof dressed in patterned tiles and its southern tower with 136-metre (446-foot) steeple known to the Viennese as 'Old Steve', the cathedral has been called the 'supreme monument of the German Gothic style'.

The beginnings of St Stephen's go back to the 12th century, when a basilica-plan church on the site was consecrated as a cathedral in the 1140s. In the 13th century it was massively rebuilt, as a vaulted hall church (with no triforium or clerestory). The nave, slightly higher than the two aisles and windowless, was begun in the 1340s. The western end is approached through a fine portal flanked by two towers, chiefly the remnants of the earlier church. The very tall southern tower which adjoins the south transept was built between about 1360 and 1435, and it was finished by the German sculptor-mason, von Prachatitz. The north tower was started in about 1450 and was completed with a cupola in the mid-16th century. The choir, of the early 14th century, is triapsidal and was to become a model for many other Austrian churches.

The interior decoration of St Stephen's is among the richest of all the central European cathedrals. There is work by Peter Parler, most notably a figure of St Paul carved in wood. The organ is by Anton Pilgram, of the early 16th century, who also decorated the pulpit with its tracery and carved heads. The high altar is by Jacob Pock, and the magnificent tomb of the Emperor Frederick III was executed by craftsmen of the school of van Leyden in the early 16th century. Some of the windows still contain original stained glass of the 15th century, which is remarkable considering the extensive damage done to Vienna during the Second World War.

St Stephen's has interesting catacombs, over 30 marble altars in the various chapels, and fragments, still visible, of the original basilican church.

Germany

Aachen

Aachen is an ancient German city where the Holy Roman Emperors were crowned from the 9th century until 1531. The cathedral does not conform to cruciform or rectangular plan, but is based upon a number of chapels erected around the Palatine Chapel built in the reign of Charlemagne (king of the Franks 768–814) as an adjunct to his sumptuous residence there.

The Palatine Chapel is a remarkable structure that has survived in much of its original state since its construction between about 798 and 805 (the year of its consecration). It is a vaulted octagonal basilica with a dome, and is surrounded by a two-storey ambulatory with galleries. It was built by Oddo of Metz under the direction of Einhard, the gifted scholar-statesman who served Charlemagne as adviser (and also wrote his biography), a many-sided genius who had studied the works of the Roman architect-engineer Marcus Vitruvius Pollio (*fl.* late 1st century B.C.-early 1st century A.D.) which were for centuries accepted as the standard authority on building design. Some of the marble columns and paving slabs were taken from ruined churches at Ravenna in Italy, capital of the western Roman Empire in the 5th century and later a major city of the Byzantine empire. Among the surviving original decorative work are grilles and doors in bronze, of very high artistic quality, and the marble throne of Charlemagne. The chapel is also the burial place of the great European ruler who was the first emperor of the Holy Roman Empire.

In the course of the next centuries there were additions. The Palatine Chapel was restored after damage by the Vikings. In the 14th century a Gothic-style chancel with choir was added and it was completed in time for consecration in 1414, the 600th anniversary of the death of Charlemagne. It was modelled upon the chancel at Sainte Chapelle in Paris (of the mid-13th century), and was given 13 26-metre (84-foot)-tall windows, tapering as they curve inwards at the top into the vaulting and separated by buttresses. The skeletal construction appears

The north aspect of Aachen Cathedral. The choir (left) is a 14th-century building leading out of the central octagonal Palatine Chapel of the 8th/9th century.

almost to be a gloriously coloured glass house with mullions. The glazing is modern, replacing the original of the 15th century. There is an interesting pulpit of bronze, decorated with precious stones, a gift of Henry II (Holy Roman Emperor 1002–24).

Cologne

If you stand at the crossing where the choir begins in St Peter's Cathedral, looking towards the glorious 46-metre (150-foot)-high east end, with its tall windows, what you see is the first building of the medieval German Gothic cathedral. This east end was begun in 1248 and the choir was consecrated in 1322. By that time the windows had been glazed with their stained glass and some of the fine sculptured statues had been erected on their corbels on the piers. Work then began on the transepts and nave, but it ground to a halt when the money ran out,

a familiar story in the history of medieval cathedrals, but in this case it was to be centuries before any further major works were undertaken again. The gigantic east end stood alone. It resembles that at Amiens, on which it was modelled, but that is not to say it was a copy, for it has two aisles on both sides, and off the ambulatory are seven radiating multangular chapels that are separated by huge double-arch flying buttresses.

After the defeat of Napoleon at Waterloo in 1815 and the resulting rearrangement of the map of Europe in which the German states recovered their integrity, there was a revival of German nationalism. One of its manifestations was a tremendous upsurge in building, wherever possible on a grand scale, and of the many projects one of the greatest was the scheme to complete St Peter's. By a happy

Rising like the proverbial phoenix from the ashes of the devastation in the Second World War, the twin spires dominate the restored western front of Cologne Cathedral, perfect in symmetry, and one of the great ecclesiastical landmarks in Europe.

The tremendous interior of Cologne Cathedral, the most majestic of the German Gothic churches. The nave is 46 metres (150 feet) tall.

chance the original design plans were rediscovered, and with influential backing, from King Frederick William III of Prussia downwards, the work was started and carried through to a triumphant conclusion. The nave was completed to a height of 46 metres (150 feet) in the style of the choir, and the two transepts were finished. The two towers on the west front had been started in the Middle Ages but had only reached the second stage. Indeed, it was recorded that the great wooden crane erected to build the south tower remained standing but idle for more than a century, as one of the sights of Cologne. Now the towers were finished and topped with two huge graceful spires of openwork tracery, soaring to a height of 157 metres (515 feet) each. The west façade, predominantly French Gothic, with three portals surmounted by tall triangular gables, was decorated with tiers of sharp-angled gables, a motif also used on the towers and the transept façades.

The overall length of the cathedral is now 143 metres (468 feet), and it is 84 metres (275 feet) wide. During the Second World War, Cologne was the victim of numerous air raids, from the earliest of the 1000-bomber attacks of 1942 right to the time of the crossing of the Rhine in 1945. Three-quarters of the city was devastated, and the cathedral was battered, burned and scarred, but it survived, as a symbol of hope to the defeated Germans after the war, and it has been restored. It still dominates the new city that continues to rise out of the ashes.

The cathedral has many priceless treasures. Among them are the life-size crucifix of Archbishop Gero of Cologne, of the 10th century, which is thought to be the oldest monumental cross surviving from the Middle Ages, and the Shrine of the Magi, a miniature church of sculptured gold in which are secreted relics of the Three Kings of the Christmas story.

Munich

This famous capital city of Bavaria, long renowned for its magnificent buildings, was sadly devastated during the Second World War. The splendid Gothic 15th-century Frauenkirche, or Church of Our Lady, that was elevated to cathedral status this century, did not escape damage, but with tremendous enthusiasm and skill it has been restored almost to its former glory. The Frauenkirche was immediately recognizable from the almost Russian ecclesiastical-style onion-topped domes on the two towers of the west façade. These have been preserved and in a city of much new building the cathedral remains a major attraction.

There was a Romanesque basilican-plan church on the site, but this was replaced in the mid-15th century by a spacious Gothic-style hall church, some 109 metres (358 feet) long. The work began in about 1470 and was completed in very quick time, about 40 years. The first architect was Jörg Ganghofer. The cathedral has a nave and two aisles of equal height, just over 30 metres (100 feet) tall. This part required major reconstruction, and today it is dazzling in its white stone, with slender octagonal columns supporting a re-creation of its fine medieval vaulted ceiling in star pattern. The high windows in the aisles are glazed with rich contemporary stained glass. The choir was also damaged, but much of the glass was preserved and is still to be seen. This was the work of Peter Hemmel (1420–1505) from Alsace, and his assistants. The choir stalls, exquisitely carved by Erasmus Grasser at the beginning of the 16th century, were not removed during the war and thus were damaged, but surviving figures have been incorporated in the rebuilt stalls. There were alterations to the cathedral in both the 18th and 19th centuries.

The western front is dominated by its two towers with their uncharacteristic onion tops, which were added in the 1520s. The towers rise to 99 metres (325 feet), and in the north tower a lift has been installed to take visitors to the top, from which there are panoramic views of the Bavarian countryside. Among the works of art are panels of an altarpiece of about 1510 which were executed by Jan Polach, considered the greatest Munich painter of the late Gothic period.

The Frauenkirche in Munich had to be substantially rebuilt after damage in the Second World War. The onion tops on the western towers, though not at all German in style, yet create an interesting contrast with the austere roof of the nave and choir.

The octagonal nave columns at Munich Frauenkirche are a rare feature in cathedral architecture, but here they are imposing without being massive.

Regensburg

Regensburg, or Ratisbon as it was known for centuries to the French, is a Bavarian city on the Danube with a long and eventful history. It was the seat of the German Diet from the 17th century to the dissolution of the Holy Roman Empire by Napoleon in 1806. Today it still has many surviving medieval buildings, among them the great German Gothic cathedral of St Peter's, begun in the 1270s upon the remains of an earlier Romanesque cathedral that dated from at least as far back as the 10th century.

St Peter's has a high nave flanked by aisles, with galleries. There are transepts but they do not protrude from the main body of the church which has slender exterior buttressing. The chancel has three windows glazed with what is regarded as some of the best 14th-century stained glass surviving in Germany. The Chapel of All Saints, which is largely a relic of the earlier cathedral, has mural and ceiling paintings.

The western front of Regensburg was begun in the late 13th century but there is doubt over the dating of various features and the order in which they were added. The two flanking towers are slightly different from one another. The south tower was begun in the 1340s and contains a very low doorway. The north tower was probably started in the mid-14th century as well. Then, in the 1360s, the mason and sculptor Wenzel Roriczer (c. 1340– c. 1420) took over the works. He is credited with the top stage of the south tower and the ogee arches and other motifs on the north and also in the centrepiece over the

Right: The cathedral of Regensburg from the south-east. The two spires at the west end were added in the 19th century.

Below: The unusual triangular central porch in the western front of Regensburg Cathedral.

A superb example of the medieval German stained-glass craftsman's skill, the Annunciation at Regensburg Cathedral.

main portal. The most attractive and unusual feature of the west front, however, is the centre porch, which projects outwards on triangular plan to give a double entrance. The centre pier has a statue of St Peter.

The tall spires of St Peter's were not added until the 1860s, but they follow Gothic style. They are of different heights.

It has been said that the west front lacks unity of style, but it is nonetheless richly carved and decorated, and the differences in the portals, arches and decoration do provide a sense of satisfaction.

Speyer

This ancient city in the Rhineland played an important role in the early history of the Reformation: indeed, the word 'Protestant' was first coined at the Diet of Speyer (or Spires) in 1529, where the Lutherans made their famous 'Protestation' against certain decisions imposed upon them. But

St Peter's Cathedral at Speyer has origins far older than that.

The cathedral was founded by Conrad II, king of Germany and emperor of the Holy Roman Empire (1024–39). It began as a basilica with a western transept and a wide, long, flat-roofed nave flanked by two vaulted aisles. Two towers were built on the sides of the choir. Another tower was raised over the central crossing, which today has an octagonal dome of later date. This building was considerably refurbished in the last years of the 11th century by Henry IV, emperor from 1056 to 1106, who converted the nave roof to vaulting, rebuilt the central crossing to give it a vault higher than the nave, and added the apsidal end. The cathedral was built from red sandstone quarried nearby, but there are arches and columns where this is alternated with bands of a whiter stone, producing an attractive contrast.

Left: The vast nave of Speyer Cathedral is groin-vaulted, with massive piers and no triforium.

The splendid eastern end of the Romanesque cathedral at Speyer, seen from the south-east. Speyer is the longest Romanesque church in central Europe.

Among the very early work is the magnificent crypt, begun in about 1030. It consists of four halls which coincide in their lateral dimensions with four parts of the cathedral above, namely, the choir, the crossing and the two transept arms. These halls below are divided by pillars surmounted by cubiform capitals that support groined vaulting. The crypt is the burial place of several Holy Roman Emperors, including Conrad II and also Rudolf I, who was the first of the Hapsburg line and died in 1291. The voussoirs in the crypt arches have the same alternating red and pinky-white banding as some of those in the main part of the cathedral.

Speyer endured a number of fires in the Middle Ages. In 1689 it was severely damaged by the French army, which set it on fire, destroying much of the nave. In the 18th century much restoration was done, faithfully in Romanesque style. The cathedral was once more badly damaged, this time in the Second World War, but has again been restored, and is one of the great Rhineland ecclesiastical masterpieces.

Trier

The cathedral at Trier could, from its western end at least, be mistaken for a fortress, with its squat but formidable central towerlike apse, flanked by two dissimilar square towers, on the oblique edge of each of which is a four-stage turret with very small windows. It is an assemblage of buildings of differing shapes and periods, forming a cathedral that straddles the site of very early buildings going back to the late Roman Empire and incorporating remains of them, notably a basilica of the reign of Emperor Gratian (375–383). Beside the cathedral and almost part of it is the Liebfrauenkirche, or Church of Our Lady, an early Gothic church of polygonal plan (built round a previous, smaller church), with an apsidal east end containing radiating chapels in the French manner.

The cathedral is basically in Romanesque style; in the centre basilica the style is grafted upon an earlier Roman nucleus which has a pediment-crowned façade to the south. In the 1040s, Archbishop Poppo of Trier began the work on the western front, which is notably for its round-headed windows and groups of round arches, enlivened by decorative niches, galleries of flat pilasters and blind arcading. The southern tower has Gothic windows in the top storey underneath a splay-foot spirelet roof. An eastern chancel with polygonal apse (over a crypt) was added in about 1160. The top

storey of the apse has a dwarf gallery. Major alterations were made to the chancel in Baroque style in the 18th century. The Romanesque nave in the basilica was vaulted in the 1220s.

Ulm

Ulm is on the Danube in Baden-Württemberg. For centuries it was a free city within the Holy Roman Empire. In the Second World War, more than half of the city was devastated by aerial bombardment, but miraculously its most famous building, the Münster, or Cathedral, with its 161-metre (528-foot) tower and spire, survived. The spire is the tallest in the world.

The Münster was begun in the 1370s and deliberately planned to accommodate a vast congregation. Designed in German Gothic style,

The western end of Trier Cathedral has marked castellar features; the bold apsidal projection seems almost to forbid approach to the two miniscule doors on either side. It is, however, a superb Romanesque front of early 11th-century origin.

Ulm has no transepts. The interior shape of the cathedral is concentrated upon its nave, choir and chancel, in line west to east. The nave has two double aisles on each side, is 125 metres (410 feet) long and rises to 42 metres (138 feet). It is a hall church, that is, the aisles are of the same height as the nave and choir, and so there is no triforium or clerestory. Inside illumination depends, therefore, on tall and wide windows in the outer aisle walls. The aisles have star-shaped lierne vaults. The choir has a magnificent set of wooden stalls carved by Jörg Syrlin the Elder between 1468 and 1474, regarded among the finest late medieval German wood sculpture in Europe. They represent two groups of people, one on either side of the choir space, biblical

characters and well-known personages from pre-Christian history.

The east end of the cathedral has two towers with octagonal cone spires flanking the apsidal end, but the dominating feature is the single tower at the western end. This is central in the western façade – and in fact takes up most of the frontage. The tower part was completed by the early 16th century, but the spire was not added until 1890, when it followed closely the scheme designed for it nearly 500 years before. In front of the tower is an interesting triple porch of three arcades screening a pair of Renaissance doors whose dividing pier (trumeau) supports a marvellous sculpture, the Man of Sorrows, by Multscher. Under the tower inside is a gallery with the

Below: The gaunt nave and choir of Ulm Cathedral (Münster), marred perhaps by the vast expanses of solid wall on either side which have to reflect the light from the small windows along the top.

Left: The tallest cathedral tower in the world, at Ulm, in floodlight. The two eastern towers have fine traceried spires. Ulm is a hall-church type of cathedral.

Right: The Münster at Basle in Switzerland, seen from the east.

Far right: The supremely colourful interior of the Baroque cathedral of St Gallen in Switzerland, decorated by Christian Wensinger.

Münster's organ of 8000 pipes and 95 stops. The top of the spire is reached by 768 steps and from it on a good day there is a tremendous view which takes in the Alps to the south.

Switzerland

Basle Münster
Resplendent in deep red sandstone on its terrace high above the Rhine in the German-speaking city of Basle, the Münster (minster) is widely regarded as the finest of all the Swiss cathedrals. Appropriately, it was the meeting place for the important Council of Basle (1431–49) which uttered the first great challenges to the supremacy of the Papacy, and when the Reformation came early in the 16th century, the city was one of its centres. Here, the great Erasmus, perhaps the supreme intellectual genius of the Revival of Learning, lived from 1521, with a short interval, until his death in 1536 and he is buried in the Münster.

The Münster, once called St Mary's, has a history going back well over 1000 years. A church was founded on the site in Carolingian times, which had three apses and whose foundations lie behind the present 14th-century choir. Its two western Romanesque towers, dissimilar in shape, were begun in about 1000. Henry II, Holy Roman Emperor from 1002 to 1024 and a dispenser of many substantial gifts to the Church, commissioned a superb golden altarpiece (later removed from Basle and now in the Musée de Cluny in Paris) which was completed in time for the cathedral's consecration in 1019.

In the late 12th century one of the richest decorated portals in Switzerland was executed at Basle by German sculptors. This is the St Gallus Portal, in Romanesque style, decorated in richly figural sculpture. Inside the cathedral, Lombardic sculptors known as the Campionesi, from Campione di Lugano, the Italian town where this school of craftsmen originated in the 12th century, worked to produce figures of apostles and

reliefs of scenes from the life of St Lawrence, a popular theme for decorated sculpture throughout the Middle Ages.

In the 13th century the west façade of the Münster began to take on a Gothic look as the fine decorated portal was completed. But in 1356 the city and countryside around were devastated by an earthquake, and the Münster was shattered. After the earthquake it was restored with strong emphasis on Swiss

Gothic style, particularly at the western end. The façade received new towers, of dissimilar shape, on the bases of the old ones, St George's tower on the north side, built between 1421 and 1429, and St Martin's, 1488–1500, on the south. Meanwhile, followers of the great German decorative sculptor and architect, Peter Parler (who worked mainly at Prague), built the choir at Basle in the 1350s and 1360s, giving it a fine glass enclosure. Here the main Council

of Basle met during those important 18 years of conference, while the subcommittees used the chapter house.

St Gallen

The abbey church of St Gallen was elevated to cathedral status in 1846. It is an elegant pinky-white basilican building in the Swiss Baroque style with some rococo decoration, built in the mid-18th century. It was designed by the great German architect, Peter

An aerial view of St Gallen Cathedral in Switzerland, a splendid 18th-century Baroque structure grafted on to remains of an early medieval monastery church that had been founded by the great Irish scholar, St Gall. The towers with their lantern-capped cupolas are at the eastern end.

Thumb (1681–1766). When you look at this graceful building, with its decorative ingenuity and yet with none of the excess so often found in Baroque styles, it is interesting to reflect that it stands upon the site of a Carolingian abbey church built in the 800s as part of the complete Benedictine monastery of St Gall, of which a parchment plan has survived from about 820.

St Gall (St Gallen in German) was an Irish hermit who in about 615 journeyed to Switzerland and built a cell in the forest land on the present site. He remained there until his death in 640. St Gall attracted many followers, and in time his simple cell blossomed into a well-organized Benedictine monastery. From the 8th to the 11th centuries, the monastery of St Gall was one of the principal repositories of learning in Europe. In the mid-

10th century it was surrounded by a fortified wall to protect it from the raids of the Saracenic Arabs.

The 18th-century church was begun in about 1755. It is built on a Latin-cross basilican plan and the main structure took some 15 years to complete, a remarkably short time. Its star features are its hall-type nave and choir with pilasters but no galleries, between which was erected a splendid rotunda. The principal façade, unusually, is at the eastern end, and is flanked by two marvellously proportioned towers of three stages, supporting ribbed cupolas that are topped with lanterns. The inside of the rotunda is decorated with superb frescoes by Christian Wensinger (1710–97). The rotunda gives the whole cathedral a dramatic sense of space, despite the relative narrowness of the nave and choir at either end.

Cathedrals of Scandinavia

Denmark

Aarhus

Aarhus is the second city of Denmark, with a long history, and St Clement's Gothic-style cathedral, the largest in Denmark, is a splendid medieval landmark among a great variety of interesting buildings. Like many Danish Gothic churches of Baltic design, notably the cathedrals of Odense and Roskilde, Aarhus Cathedral is built of brick. It was started at the very end of the 12th century or the beginning of the 13th by its founder, Bishop Peder Vognsen, who died in about 1204, upon the remains of an earlier Romanesque church that had been built in stone, almost the same size. The nave of St Clement's is the longest in the

The cathedral at Aarhus in Denmark, from the south. The octagonal steeple rises to over 94 metres (310 feet) and is a 20th-century addition.

country, almost 93 metres (305 feet), and the cathedral has one of the handsomest steeples, rising out of an imposing square west tower. This was completed in the 1920s, and rises to over 94 metres (310 feet).

Inside, the tall, lengthy nave is flanked by aisles barely half the nave's height. The transepts have no aisles but are as tall as the nave. On the exterior, the gable ends of the transepts are stepped. The choir is three-aisled, and it was added in the 15th century. The magnificent high altar is by Bernt Notke (1430–1509), the German-born artist from Lübeck, who also painted an important triptych and whose assistants produced much of the fresco painting. In the chancel there is a black marble slab covering the tomb of the founder.

St Clement's Cathedral was ravaged by fire on several occasions and so has had to sustain much rebuilding. Yet it remains a marvellous example of medieval Danish brick building work. Much of the interior sculpture and decoration was by stone-cutters from Zealand and Jutland, notably Mikkel van Groningen who carved the great pulpit in the 1580s, and by Quellinus the Younger (1661–1709), the Belgian artist who produced sombre yet vibrant funerary monuments in white and black marble. The cathedral organ was installed in the 1730s, and was rebuilt in the 1920s to specifications set out by Albert Schweitzer, the world-famous philosopher, healer and musical scholar, a leading authority on organ technology.

Roskilde

Capital of Denmark throughout most of the Middle Ages, residence and ultimate resting place of Danish kings and queens, Roskilde has one of the greatest of

Left: The brick-walled nave of Aarhus's Gothic cathedral is whitewashed.

Right: The Lutheran cathedral in Helsinki, Finland, stands on granite rock above Senate Square in the old part of the city. It is in neo-classical style and was begun in the 1830s.

Below: The western front of the brick-built cathedral of Roskilde in Denmark is austere and angular. The spires were raised in the 17th century.

the cathedrals of Denmark. Begun as a small stone church in the early 11th century, it was consecrated in 1084. This early building did not, however, survive, and when in about 1190 Bishop Peder Suneson, who had studied in France and presumably visited several French cathedrals, began to build a new cathedral at Roskilde in pink brick upon the foundations of the earlier church, fragments of which have survived, he gave it a French plan: late Romanesque with three aisles, and a choir with an ambulatory similar to that at Tournai in Belgium.

In the 13th and 14th centuries the cathedral was enlarged and greatly modified in Gothic style, also in the French manner, but without obscuring the Romanesque, so that the whole resembles the ordered merging of one style into the other. The western façade was flanked with double towers, whose slender spires were added in the 17th century.

Roskilde Cathedral is the burial place of the kings and queens of Denmark, and much of the interior decorative work is devoted to chapels set aside to their memory, and to sarcophagi and

other royal monuments, many of them in marble and alabaster which are set off well by the red and white colouring of the interior. One of the foremost monuments is the black marble tomb of Queen Margaret, who united Norway with Denmark and ruled them from 1387 until her death in 1412. The tomb was executed in the 1420s, and is an outstanding example of Gothic sculpture, executed by Johannes Junge of Lübeck. There are also fine monuments by Cornelis de Vriendt (Cornelis Floris, who also worked at Tournai). The chapel commemorating Frederick V (king of Denmark and Norway 1746–66) is the work of C. F. Harsdorff (1735–99), who was professor of architecture at the Copenhagen Academy of Fine Arts.

Sweden

Lund

Begun in the 1080s, Lund is one of the oldest cathedrals in Scandinavia. The major work on it was carried out in the 12th century, and considerable restoration was undertaken in the 19th century, yet it is still essentially Romanesque. Built largely in limestone, it has distinctive Lombardic features, notably the rich sculptures on the capitals and mouldings of the famous crypt.

A cathedral of simple nave, aisle and choir in Anglo-Saxon style was started in the time of Canute IV (king of Denmark 1080–86), who sponsored it. About 1100, it was remodelled by a master mason called Donatus (who died c. 1130), and then by his successor, another mason, Regnerus (d. 1160s). They converted the cathedral into a substantial basilican building, with nave, choir leading to rounded apsidal east end, and transepts with square chapels attached to the east side of each, abutting on to the choir. There is no triforium to the nave and the clerestory has very limited windows, restricting the light inside. The apsidal end, with its two tiers of blind arcade exterior decoration crowned by an eaves gallery, is one of the most distinctive Lombardic features in any Scandinavian church, the work of artists and masons from central Italy.

While the building was rising upwards from ground level, a magnificent crypt was simultaneously being erected

The remarkable Romanesque cathedral at Lund, with its great apsidal east end, was for centuries the coronation church of the Swedish kings.

Right: Uppsala Cathedral, an early Gothic building, was much restored in the 19th century. The western spires are almost 120 metres (390 feet) tall.

Far right: Inside the Gothic cathedral at Uppsala in Sweden the overall impression is of controlled space. Tall, with no triforium, the nave rises to a fine vaulted roof.

underneath. It is groin-vaulted throughout, supported upon rows of interestingly varied columns topped by cushion capitals. It was completed by about 1135. Some of the foundations of the 11th-century church are preserved. In the 13th century, two towers were added to the western façade which has since been altered.

In the 14th and 15th centuries, the cathedral was adorned with decorative work of many kinds.

The wood carving on the choir stalls, of the 1380s, was influenced by Peter Parler. The high altar by the school of the north-west German master, Bertram, was executed at the end of the 14th century. In the late 15th century and early 16th, the German, Adam van Düren, worked at the cathedral and produced the tomb of Archbishop Birger Gunnarsson.

Lund Cathedral was damaged by fire in the 1230s, and

afterwards the nave was restored with a vaulted roof. In the 16th century, Lund was left to decay, partly because of the Reformation. But restoration work of the 19th century brought the cathedral back to its Romanesque glory. The Lombardic south portal arch, in particular, was restored with care and feeling.

Uppsala

The cathedral at Uppsala is the largest in Scandinavia. It also has the least typically Scandinavian features, for it was designed by a French architect and built in the French Gothic style, which was maintained when it was restored in the 1880s–1890s by a Swedish architect.

The first cathedral of the bishops of Uppsala was built in about 1100 at Old Uppsala, near the site of a splendid 9th-century heathen temple 'which gleamed with gold'. The cathedral was destroyed by fire and the bishopric, which had been advanced to an archbishopric, was moved 2 miles (3 kilometres) south to the present city, then known as Ostra Aros. In the later part of the 13th century the French architect, Etienne de Bonneuil, who had worked at Notre-Dame in Paris, was invited to plan a new cathedral. (A French record of about 1287 says that Bonneuil had been sent '*faire l'église de Upsal*'.) The first work was done in cut stone, but from the 14th century brick was used instead. Unusually for a medieval cathedral, Uppsala was erected largely in one main operation, although that stretched over more than a century (Salisbury in England is another one-operation structure).

The cathedral has two side aisles to its nave, with many chapels between the buttresses on north and south, transepts, and a choir with ambulatory and radiating chapels. The easternmost chapel in the apsidal end has the mausoleum of the great Gustavus Vasa (king of Sweden 1523–60), founder of the royal house of Vasa, who was educated at Uppsala University (founded 1477). It is the work of Guillaume Boyers, one of the leading Dutch Renaissance artists

working in Sweden in the 1570s. Near the high altar is the Coronation Vault, under which many of the kings of Sweden were crowned.

Uppsala was consecrated in 1435. By that time it had its fine western doorway, with two small towers flanking it, which were later heightened – and later still (19th century) given spires sheathed in copper to reach a height of 119 metres (389 feet). These enable the cathedral to be seen from a great distance. During the 15th century the sculpture workshop at Uppsala became the centre of late Gothic sculpture throughout Sweden.

The interior of Uppsala is lofty and exciting, with slender clustered columns topped with small, dainty capitals, emphasizing the height. The restoration work of Helgo Zettervall (1831–1907) has been criticized for its heaviness but it has preserved faithfully the essential medieval character of the cathedral.

Left: The octagonal Chapel of St Olaf at the eastern end of Trondheim Cathedral. Much of the cathedral has been reconstructed during the past century but in keeping with its medieval Gothic origin.

Right: The splendidly ornate Gothic nave of Trondheim Cathedral, extensively restored in the 19th and 20th centuries.

Norway

Trondheim

Little more than 200 miles (330 kilometres) south of the Arctic Circle in Norway is Trondheim city, dominated by Scandinavia's finest cathedral. At 99 metres (326 feet) from east to west, the cathedral is also Scandinavia's largest. Extensively altered and restored because of numerous fires and other catastrophes, Trondheim still retains the essential mixture of Romanesque with English and French Gothic influences that helped to create it in the 12th and 13th centuries.

Trondheim was known in the Middle Ages as Nidaros Cathedral. Begun in about 1130 as a church in the Anglo-Norman manner, its principal feature of this period was the majestic transepts of about 1150. The design was changed later in the century after a long visit to England in the 1180s by its archbishop, Eystein Erlandson. From then on it began to change into Gothic style. In Eystein's time the sacristy on the north side of the choir was completed, along with a Lady Chapel with ribbed vaulting, and the famous octagonal chapel was begun. This huge chapel, at the end of the long choir, was built to house the grave of St Olaf (Olaf II, king of Norway 1016–28), who converted Norway to Christianity, and it was finished in the 1250s. The original one-aisled choir of the 12th century was replaced by a much grander three-aisled choir in the Early English manner at the beginning of the 13th century. The nave, still the most glorious feature of the whole cathedral, was begun in the 1240s. Some architectural historians compare it with the Angel Choir at Lincoln.

By the 14th century Trondheim Cathedral was largely complete, except for its west façade and its three portals, which had been started. A succession of disasters over the next centuries, fires, sieges and storms, interrupted any sustained building work. Indeed, it is believed that for a long time it had no roof. Moreover, there was further spoliation at the time of the Reformation. But in the last century, as part of the growth of Norwegian national assertion, an extensive restoration programme was begun, culminating in its superb medieval look today.

Cathedrals of the Mediterranean

Spain

Burgos

One of the finest Spanish Gothic cathedrals, Burgos seems to rise out of the side of the hill on which the city stands, and as you go up towards it, you find you have to use ramps and steps. On its north side, the street level is above the door into the western façade. It is a Gothic masterpiece, with tremendous emphasis on exterior decoration, and yet it is breathtaking inside too.

The cathedral was begun in the early 1220s under the patronage of Ferdinand III (king of Castile 1217–52). By the 1230s, enough had been built to enable the first services to be held, and this appears to have included the lower parts of the nave, transepts and chancel with apse, ambulatory and radiating chapels. The first mason in charge was probably one Ricardo, and he was followed in the 1240s by Enrique, a French master who had worked on León Cathedral. By 1260 the nave and transepts were complete, and perhaps the chapels too, and this date is given by some authorities for the cathedral's consecration which Ferdinand did not live to see. By this time, too, the western façade had been started, along with the bases of two flanking towers. Then the work slowed down.

In the 15th century, the top half of the cathedral's exterior began to receive the amazingly intricate and handsome treatment that has distinguished it ever since. In pure Gothic decoration, Hans of Cologne (1410–81), a German-born master mason who called himself Juan de Colonia in Spain, finished the top stages of the towers and their spires between 1442 and 1458. His son, Simón, built on to the end of the chancel at the east (1482–94) a fantastic chapel, the Capillo del Condestable (Constable's Chapel) for Pedro Hernández de Velasco, hereditary constable of Castile. This extraordinary structure, octagonal, with eight pinnacles surmounting the roof and its balustraded parapet, was gloriously decorated internally with sculpture, figures of Christ, saints, and coats of arms with their supporters. The roof was vaulted with wonderful petal-like design; stained glass flooded the windows and the vault centre.

The octagonal Capillo del Condestable (Constable's Chapel), one of the supreme decorative glories of the Spanish Gothic cathedral at Burgos. Behind the altar is a huge and remarkable retable carved in the Plateresque style by de Vigarni and Diego de Siloé.

Simón's son, Francisco, built the splendid central lantern (1540–68) whose exterior has 12 pinnacles set round a rich latticework balustrade that 'curves and twists round the octagon'.

There are chapels encircling the cathedral in a variety of individual styles, which cannot be described here. The cathedral itself is a pure delight; over 106 metres (350 feet) long and 58 metres (190 feet) at its widest, it is a virtual treasure house of sculpture and carving by famous artists, among them de Siloé, de Vigarni and de Vallejo, all major creative men of their age.

Murcia

Murcia lies on the river Segura in the south-east of Spain, about 20 miles (30 kilometres) inland. Its cathedral, originally Gothic and built between 1394 and the last decades of the 15th century, was radically altered by some 16th-century additions and again as a result of major work in the 18th century following a terrible flooding of the Segura in 1735. Among the earlier features still in fine preservation are the octagonal chapel of the Vélez family (c. 1455–1510) in the south-east, which has a beautiful screen and star vaulting, and the Puerta de las Cadenas (Door of the Chains) of 1512–15, in the north side, executed by Juan de León.

In 1520, work started on Murcia's dominating north tower, which was not completed until the end of the 18th century. It rises to just under 90 metres (300 feet), and is distinctive in having the appearance of a 'drawn-out telescope', in five diminishing storeys. Several well-known artists worked on the tower over the two centuries or so, notably Jerónimo Quijano (from 1526 to 1546), who

The profile of Burgos Cathedral commands a view to the hills in the distance. On the right are the twin towers of the western façade, in the centre, the tower over the crossing, and on the left, the marvellous octagon of the Constable's Chapel.

also designed the Junterones Chapel in what is called the Plateresque style.

The major change to the cathedral, however, was the 18th-century addition of a splendid western façade, described by Sacheverell Sitwell as a masterpiece of 'decadent' architecture. This is in Baroque style and was constructed between 1736 and 1755 as part of the restoration after the floods. It was designed by Jaime Bort and its principal feature is its broad central niche within a pyramidal superstructure with hooded frontispiece, which appears as if it is propped up from behind 'like the proscenium of a toy theatre'. This 'proscenium' is richly decorated with statues in smaller niches, sculptures of winged angels, blind balustrades, columns and cartouches.

The inside of the cathedral still retains its Gothic look, with ogee arches, but here and there are fine Renaissance features, notably the Baptistery of the late 1530s.

New Cathedral, Salamanca

About a quarter of a mile (half a kilometre) north of the river Tormes in Salamanca, and immediately adjacent to the old Romanesque cathedral built in the 12th century, is the New Cathedral (Catedral Nueva). It is an impressive Gothic structure begun in about 1513, and still being worked on in the 18th century. It is remarkable for its profusely decorated western façade, an extravagant example of late Gothic work, and for its lofty south-west tower of about 110 metres (360 feet), raised in the 16th century and sheathed in masonry following the terrible earthquake in Lisbon in 1755.

Salamanca New Cathedral was designed by Juan Gil de Hontañón following an invitation by Bishop de Bobadilla in 1512 to all the leading architects in Spain to submit plans. Hontañón worked on the cathedral until his death, when he was followed by his son, Rodrigo. It stands on a hill above the river, and like the

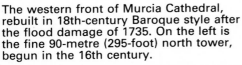

The western front of Murcia Cathedral, rebuilt in 18th-century Baroque style after the flood damage of 1735. On the left is the fine 90-metre (295-foot) north tower, begun in the 16th century.

great cathedral at Segovia it has an imposing nave, Renaissance-style towers flanking the western façade, with cupolas and lanterns, and a square eastern end. The south-west tower was designed by Rodrigo and is modelled upon the Gothic north-west tower of the previous century at Toledo. Over the central crossing is a fine cupola that was not finished until the 1730s. It was designed by José and Joaquín Churriguera.

The western façade is a marvellous example of the richest kind of Gothic exterior decorative work. The portals are covered with statues, busts and coats of arms, in the rich yellow-gold stone quarried nearby. The north portal, known as the Puerta de las Palmas, which opens on to the Plaza de Anaya, has a relief tableau of Christ's entry into Jerusalem. The façade of the north transept is dominated by many pinnacles.

Inside the cathedral, which is almost 105 metres (340 feet) long and 50 metres (160 feet) wide at the transepts, the nave is skirted by a balustrade supported on moulded piers. There is a traceried gallery round the aisles and transepts. The choir, not

The New Cathedral at Salamanca with its Renaissance towers was built in the 16th century right beside the earlier Romanesque cathedral, on the hill above the river Tormes (in the foreground). The bridge was constructed in Roman times.

73

completed until the 1730s, is in Churrigueresque style.

Among the treasures of the cathedral is a Byzantine bronze crucifix which was carried into battle by El Cid (The Champion), otherwise Rodrigo Díaz de Bivar (1040–99), the celebrated medieval Spanish hero who fought for various Spanish and Moorish rulers in the Iberian peninsula. The crucifix came to Salamanca with Bishop Jerónimo, El Cid's confessor, who incidentally founded the older cathedral.

Santiago de Compostela

Sacheverell Sitwell called this cathedral 'one of the most splendid fantastic buildings in the world'. And well he might, for as you come into the Plaza de España, the city's central square, you cannot fail to be astonished, perhaps overwhelmed, by the sight of the cathedral of St James (Santiago) the Great. The exterior is almost entirely Baroque, in the most exuberant manifestation of this interesting style in Spain. Fronting on to the square is the

Obradoiro, that is, the western façade, which is reached by means of a double external staircase climbing in two flights. The façade, a vast centrepiece with wings, adorned with Corinthian pillars, is built in stages up to a top-level statue of St James. Flanking the façade are two towers, rising in diminishing stages to a high cupola. This amazing frontispiece is the work of Fernando Casas y Nóvoa and dates from between 1738 and 1749. Other Baroque features are more façades on south and north transepts, not finished until the 1770s.

If you think you will now be going into a Baroque interior, as soon as you pass through the vast double doors of the Obradoiro you find a completely different style – Romanesque. This is the original cathedral, built in the 11th and 12th centuries. Even part of the original west façade is still there, the magnificent Portico de la Gloria, a Romanesque triple portico with exquisite sculpture executed by Master Mateo in the

years 1168–88. Go through this and you are in the enormous 11–bay nave of the early 12th century, barrel-vaulted and 22 metres (72 feet) high, with cross-vaulted side aisles, in total 18 metres (59 feet) across. There is no clerestory, which limits the illumination, but the triforium is deep, with double-arched openings. All in all it is an austere and simple nave. The transepts have aisles and two round apses each eastern side. The choir is enclosed by an ambulatory with five radiating chapels leading off a rounded east end. The high altar is much later, in Churrigueresque style. The whole interior is 94 metres (310 feet) long.

The cathedral was for centuries a major place of pilgrimage, often described as second only to Rome. This is because it is built on the site of a much smaller church which had been raised in the 9th century to contain the bones of St James, one of Christ's 12 disciples. His body was encased in a stone coffin, and it had been discovered near the city in 813.

These relics are now in a marble coffin in the shrine of St James.

Santiago is built mainly of local yellow and grey stone. The octagonal lantern was erected in the late 14th and early 15th centuries.

Segovia

This marvellously constructed yellow-gold-hued cathedral is the last major Gothic creation in Spain. Sited on the hill in Segovia city, overlooking the famous Alcázar and near the Roman aqueduct, the cathedral presents on its eastern side a fascinating aspect of several stages (or steps) of building rising to the lantern on the cupola over the central crossing. Overlooking it all is the lofty tower flanking the western façade.

Segovia was begun in 1522 on the site of an earlier cathedral destroyed in an insurrection. Designed by Juan Gil de Hontañón and his son Rodrigo, who also built the New Cathedral at Salamanca, it is Spanish Gothic, richly decorated and beautifully ornate, with pointed arches and delicate but firm flying buttresses. Pinnacles and pierced balustrading provide further adornment.

The cathedral was constructed principally in the 70 or so years between 1522 and 1595. The plan is basilican, and the cathedral has

no transepts. It ends at the east in a corona of seven radiating polygonal chapels leading out of an apsidal chancel which emerges from the choir. The chancel is Baroque, decorated by Manuel de Churriguera. Over the crossing is a substantial cupola on square base, 67 metres (220 feet) high and capped with a lantern and small spire. The nave, supported on tall, slim clustered shafts, is flanked by chapels, most of them screened, and in place of the triforium is a gallery with pierced balustrade. The marvellous stained glass and the rich golden stone create an elevating effect on the tall vaulting of nave and aisles.

The western front is plain and simple, and on its south-west angle is the 105-metre (345-foot)-tall square-plan tower, with pilaster buttresses and domed lantern which was raised in the 1620s.

Seville

One wonders what Julius Caesar, the greatest man in history, who founded a Roman colony at Seville in 45 B.C., would have thought of Seville Cathedral. Begun in the early 1400s under the supervision of a French master mason, it rose to become the biggest medieval cathedral in the world.

It was built on the site of a major Moorish mosque which was pulled down to make room. The only building left standing was the minaret, the square-plan brick and stone tower of 1184–98, 16 metres (54 feet) square with 2·5-metre (8-foot)-thick walls, to which was added, three and a half centuries later, the Renaissance-style belfry and revolving figure on top, hence the name the Giralda, from the Spanish 'girar', 'to revolve'. The new works followed approximately the ground plan of the mosque, and covered a vast rectangle 131 metres (430 feet) from east to west and 76 metres (250 feet) from north to south, not including the Patio de los Naranjos, the court of the old mosque on the north side. The cathedral is built horizontally rather than vertically, and has neither domes nor towers (except

Above: The largest medieval cathedral in Europe, Seville Cathedral in southern Spain. Its only tower is the Renaissance-style belfry known as the Giralda.

Right: The superbly proportioned interior of Seville Cathedral, whose nave is 40 metres (130 feet) tall, supported on what seem very slender piers.

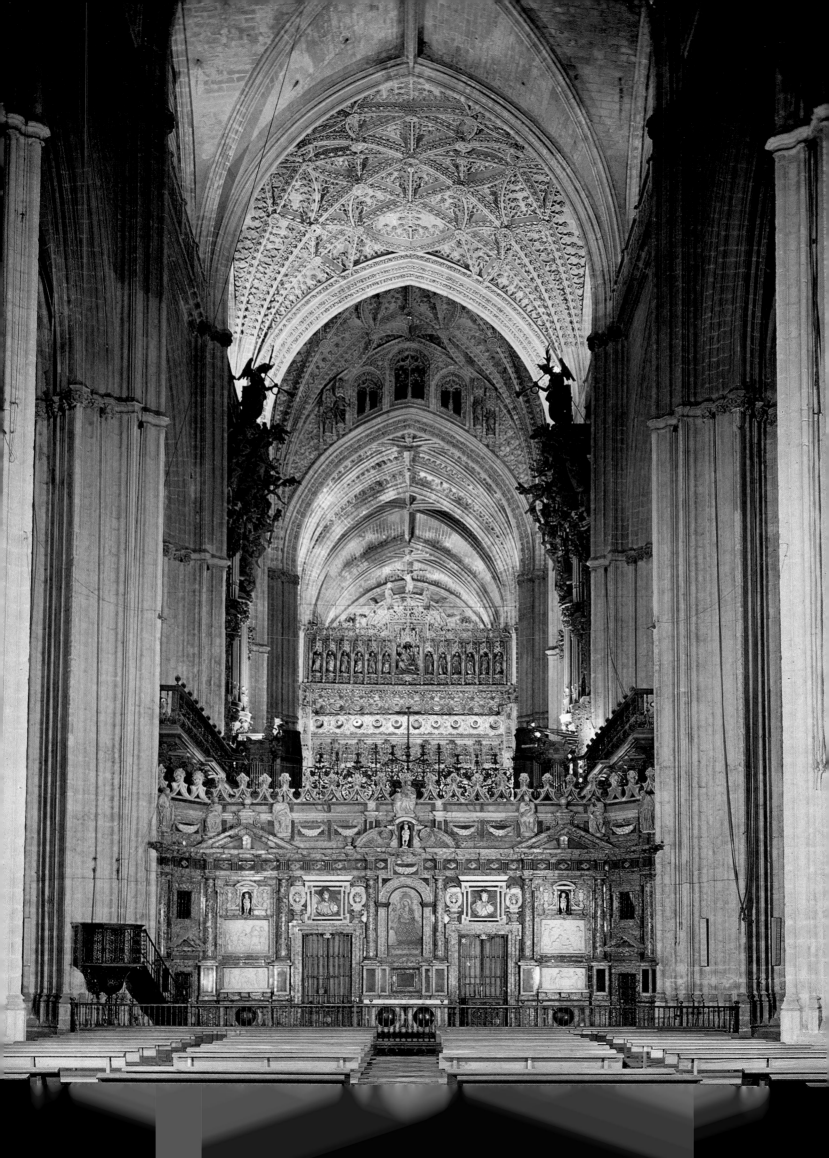

the Giralda), yet its interior is breathtaking, chiefly because of its wide nave with 40-metre (130-foot)-high quadripartite vaulting supported on immense clustered piers with foliated capitals, flanked by double aisles on both sides on equally towering piers. There is no triforium, but a balustraded gallery rises to the clerestory which has glorious stained glass beautifully framed in curvilinear tracery. There is a central lantern with a star vault. It was first raised in the 15th century, collapsed in 1511, was reconstructed in 1519 by Juan Gil de Hontañón (who worked on the New Cathedral at Salamanca), collapsed again in the 1880s, and was rebuilt once more

The enormous and interesting west façade of Toledo Cathedral combines Romanesque, Gothic and Renaissance styles.

The east end of Seville Cathedral terminates centrally with the Capilla Real (Chapel Royal) with a rounded apse and curved ends, built between 1550 and 1575, and it contains the tomb of Ferdinand III of Castile, who died in 1252, set in a silver and bronze shrine. The entrance to the cathedral today is through a small doorway with arch, squashed almost between the Capilla Real and the Giralda. But there are decorated façades with portals on the other three sides, the western façade having three portals flanked by fine sculptures by Mercadante and Millán.

The inside of Seville is practically surrounded by chapels along the inner walls, each of them containing important works of art, notably some by Murillo, Valdés Leal and Jordaens. By the south transept is a monument to Columbus, erected in 1899 when his remains were brought back from Cuba. There is a mass of superb ironwork, grilles, gates, pulpits and lecterns, fabricated by the leading Spanish ironsmiths, including works by Francisco de Salamanca. The floor of the cathedral had originally been laid in brick, but in the late 18th century it was taken up and replaced with fine marble paving.

Toledo

Toledo Cathedral is a worthy building for the primate of Spain. It is also an outstanding feature of the ancient city which is now a national monument, and it probably houses more distinguished works of art than any other cathedral in Spain, including many major paintings by Goya, Titian, Bellini and Giordano, as well as by El Greco who made his home in Toledo and died there in the early 17th century.

The design of Toledo, though basically of French 13th-century Gothic inspiration, is an unusual one in many respects. It has no transepts projecting from the main rectangle of the church; they stop at the portals on north and south sides. A variety of chapels and sacristy buildings appear tacked on to the main building. There is a cloister on the north flank of the nave, and you have to enter the cathedral by means of a door in the west arm of the cloister, proceed eastwards to a portal along the north wall of the nave and go down a flight of stairs into the northernmost aisle. The north tower flanking the façade is a magnificent Gothic structure rising in five stages to a lantern topped by a spire, overall 90 metres (295 feet) tall, but the south tower begins as a square, changes to octagonal and finishes up as a dome, under which is a chapel designed by El Greco's son (1631). But withal, we are considering one of the finest and most beautiful Gothic buildings in Europe.

Toledo began in the 1220s on the site of a 6th-century church founded by St Eugenius, first bishop of Toledo, which was converted into a mosque when the Moors took Toledo in the 7th century. Recovered in the late 11th century, the church was later dismantled by Ferdinand III to inaugurate the new structure. Work started on the east end, which is apsidal, with a double ambulatory off which leads a variety of chapels of different shapes. The nave, however, is the dominant feature of the interior, austere, lofty, seven-bayed, with double aisles. It has tall, clustered-shaft piers topped with foliate capitals supporting the pointed-arch vaulting, with a fine clerestory still glazed with much of its original 13th-century and 14th-century stained glass, but there is no triforium. As with most Spanish cathedrals, the choir is to the west of the crossing, and here there is a veritable museum of sculpture in wood, stone, bronze and iron. East of the choir is the Capilla Mayor (chancel) where the high altar has an amazing Gothic retable of larchwood, carved, painted and gilded during the first years of the 16th century, and depicting scenes from the life of Christ.

The western façade is chiefly 15th-century, with beautifully sculptured, deeply recessed portals in the French style. The north tower, built between 1380 and 1440, was topped with its lantern and spire in the mid-15th century, by the Belgian craftsman Anequín de Egas. There is one

feature of Toledo that has attracted a mixture of unqualified praise and savage criticism. It is *El Transparente,* a fantastic marble sculpture, a 'theatrical *trompe l'œil'* of the 1730s by Narciso Tomé. This tableau situated to the east of the chancel begins at the top with a group of cherubim, then a Christ in glory above a scene from the Last Supper, under which is a bursting sun whose rays spill over the Virgin and Child at the bottom. To heighten the effect of this extraordinary Baroque monument, which is in Churrigueresque style, the architect opened a hole in one of the panels in the stone vaulting of the roof and glazed it to let in the sun.

One of the supreme achievements of Churrigueresque art, *El Transparente,* behind the high altar in Toledo Cathedral, is also among the most controversial examples of this Spanish Baroque creative style.

Far right: The austere nave of Florence Cathedral is well lit by medallion windows at clerestory level, an illumination tempered by reflection from the polychrome marble floor.

Right: The fortress-cathedral of Sé Velha at Coimbra in Portugal, seen from the south-west. The two portals seem more appropriate to a castle.

Portugal

Coimbra

The grand old 12th-century cathedral of Sé Velha at Coimbra is the best preserved in Portugal. Looking more like a fortress from some angles – stark rectilinear transepts with thick walls and battlements like great towers, little window space and arrow loops in the eastern apses – Sé Velha is nevertheless the best example of Portuguese Romanesque ecclesiastical architecture, and it is dramatically enhanced by its position high on the hill in the city. Understandably, architectural historians have waxed enthusiastic about its features.

Sé Velha was a 10th-century church which in the 1160s began to be rebuilt as a basilican-plan cathedral providing a place of pilgrimage. The design was heavily influenced by ideas employed in the Auvergne region of France, and French masons masterminded the work in the earlier years, for some of the time under Master Bernardo (*fl.* 12th century). The east end has three apses, parallel but not in line, the two outer ones oddly asymmetrical. There is a lantern top to the southern apse. Over the crossing is a broad, square tower with polygonal corners, rising to a fine ribbed cupola with Byzantine-style ceramic tiling, and this is capped by a lantern. The tower, which is rib-vaulted, is lit by double round-headed windows that flood the crossing with light. The nave is barrel-vaulted with transverse arches and is flanked by two vaulted aisles, each surmounted by a wide gallery. The western end terminates in a façade which is austere but has a beautifully sculptured round-headed portico with typical Romanesque motifs. This is reached by a flight of steps. On the north side of the cathedral, almost midway between the north transept and the western end, is a second portal, in fine Renaissance style, and this was added in the early 16th century.

Inside the cathedral there is some of the most exquisite carving and sculpture to be found in Portugal. Some of the medieval tombs and the Manueline baptismal font are notable. There is a glorious retable (1498–1503) in gilded and polychrome wood, by the Flemish artist, Olivier de Gand. De Gand was the first of a number of artists and sculptors to work at Coimbra in the Renaissance period, making it, for much of the 16th century, the leading sculptural centre in Portugal, where craftsmen trained and from which they went out to work at other great buildings. The chapels of St Peter and the Sacrament were decorated in the mid-16th century in a blend of French and Portuguese styles.

Italy

Cefalù, Sicily

Rising out of the mountainside, sheer beside the sea in northern Sicily, Cefalù is an astonishing Siculo-Norman cathedral, with clear Saracenic and Byzantine features, built in a lovely golden limestone that glistens in the Mediterranean sun. The great Roger II, Norman ruler of Sicily (and part of southern Italy), first as count (1105–30) and then as king (1130–54), initiated its building in 1131 and it was completed by 1150. It is a stark, bold fortress-like cathedral, distinctive at almost every point from east to west.

Cefalù was built with nave (with single aisles), transepts, and presbytery with internally rounded apsidal end (polygonal on the outside). Transepts and presbytery are reinforced on the exterior by narrow but formidable pilaster buttresses such as are found on the great towers of numerous Norman castles (for example Falaise, Hedingham and Richmond, among others), but with blind interlaced arcading round the top of the walls. The inside is lit by narrow Saracenic pointed-arch windows and by oculi (rounded openings). The transepts and presbytery are lofty, a tallness accentuated by the full height of the apse. In the angles between the transepts and presbytery are side apses, similarly rounded. The timber-roofed nave is considerably lower in height, its aisles are cross-vaulted, and its western end is squashed, as it were, between two formidable west towers between which is also the vaulted portico whose central arch is round-headed, with pointed arches on either side.

This remarkable cathedral, Norman and Saracenic in its outer appearance, reveals its Byzantine glories once you are in the brilliantly decorated presbytery end. The half-dome of the apsidal end bears a magnificent 12th-century mosaic of Christ Pantocrator, giving his blessing and at the same time drawing the observer's eye to the open pages of a book, in gold and blue. The vaulting above contains cherubim and seraphim, and in the curved wall of the apse, in tiered panels, are the Virgin Mary between angels, and below her in two rows, the apostles. These mosaics form a dramatic highlight to the main altar which is in the apse.

The walls, windows, cornices and arches are covered in richly coloured mosaics, which were executed between 1148 and 1170, chiefly by local craftsmen, but which are of high quality.

The cathedral is over 73 metres (240 feet) long, with transepts nearly 30 metres (100 feet) wide, and is dedicated to St Saviour.

Florence

The great cathedral of Santa Maria del Fiore was built between 1296 and 1461. It was raised by the growingly adventurous and prosperous Florentines to replace their older, smaller cathedral of Santa Reparata, though they retained the older church's fine baptistery, a separate octagonal three-storeyed building of 5th–century origins, faced with contrasting dark green and white marble in the 11th century. The new cathedral was designed initially by Arnolfo di Cambio, with Romanesque and Gothic features. The plan consisted of a

long, wide nave with single aisle on each side, leading to a three-storey central octagon, and the work was well under way by 1300.

The western façade was begun in the early 14th century, with three tall, slender portals corresponding in position with the nave and aisles. This façade was unfortunately pulled down in 1588, but we know of its design by Arnolfo, and the shape it took, from a surviving picture now in the cathedral museum. A new façade was completed in the 1880s by Emilio De Fabris.

How Arnolfo determined to cover the octagon is not known, but it is clear that he intended the north, east and south sides of it to be flanked with smaller semi-octagonal two-storey chapels with dome roofs, as they have been. Arnolfo died in about 1310 and work came to a halt.

Twenty-four years later, the great artist Giotto was commissioned to design the campanile, to be erected on the

south-west corner but detached from it, and he saw the tower built to its second storey. It was continued by his pupil, Andrea Pisano, and when it was completed by Francesco Talenti in 1359, it was 99 metres (325 feet) high. In the same year, work was resumed on the cathedral, and it is recorded that the plans, including the revisions considered necessary, were discussed at great length in public. By 1420 the nave was complete and an octagonal drum had been raised as a top storey to the octagon, ready to receive a dome. The octagon was 42 metres (138 feet) across. At this stage, the Florentine architect, Filippo Brunelleschi, one of the greatest of all the Renaissance architects, who had begun his career as a goldsmith and sculptor, was commissioned, after a lot of haggling over his initial proposals, to construct a dome, and with astonishing ingenuity and boldness he seized upon the Gothic technical

The choir and presbytery of the Romanesque cathedral of Cefalù in Sicily watched over by Christ Pantocrator in glorious, rich-coloured Byzantine mosaic in the half-dome of the eastern apse. In front is the first of the quadripartite-vaulted bays of the choir.

innovation of the ribbed vault and built a ribbed 'cage', taller than a hemisphere, which he used to support an outer dome of brick panels tied to a second, inner dome. This enabled him to dispense with reinforcing the octagonal drum. The lantern above was designed by him but not erected until after his death in 1446.

During his years at Florence, Brunelleschi supervised the continuation of other works, and by the time of his death the cathedral was largely complete. The exterior was veneered in red, green and white marble, some by this time, the remainder within the century. It was a triumphant conclusion and Florence had a cathedral that was to be, until the building of St Peter's in Rome, the largest cathedral in Italy, a worthy symbol of the power and accomplishments of the Florentine Republic, its wealth, its artistic genius and its intellectual influence.

The interior is relatively austere, but noble and majestic. It contains few great sculptures, but among them is an unfinished Descent from the Cross by Michelangelo, dated 1547–55.

Milan

One could be forgiven for looking upon Milan Cathedral as Gothic gone mad. Certainly, it is an astonishing structure, huge (one of the largest cathedrals in the world), gaunt and lofty inside, decorated outside with a forest of gables and arches, and of pinnacles reaching into the sky. Rich with statuary, it gleams with its white marble dressing upon a largely brick core.

Milan was started in the 1380s under Simone da Orsenigo, described as engineer and general master, upon a site where there were several churches and other buildings, including the old cathedral of Santa Maria Maggiore which had been sacked in 1162 and not restored. The new cathedral was designed on cruciform plan. The first works went up round the remains of the older cathedral, and they were bedevilled with difficulties. The ruler of Milan refused to support the project and money had to come from public subscription which was not always reliable. The Italians, having decided upon Gothic, consulted French and German specialists and then declined to take all their advice. The ambulatory and the short double-aisled transepts seemed acceptable, but they baulked at side chapels in the nave and objected to exterior sloping roofs for nave and transepts, which received flat, marble-tiled roofs.

There were more problems. In 1487, for example, having decided to cover the central crossing with a cupola, the authorities invited Leonardo da Vinci and Bramante to provide designs, and promptly rejected them. Then the scheme was thrown open to competition, which was won by Giovanni Amadeo and Giovanni Dolcebono, pupils of Bramante, in 1490, and in the last years of the 15th century work on the cupola was begun.

In the 1650s, the western front was begun in Gothic style, but it was not completed until the 19th century, and only then because Napoleon, who had crushed the Austrians at Marengo in 1800 and created a Cisalpine Republic in North Italy, ordered the work to be hastened. The lantern over the cupola had been designed by Amadeo in the 1490s, but it was not finished, along with its 107-metre (350-foot) spire, until 1750.

The nave, begun in the 15th century, was not completed until the 16th century. It is nine-bayed, with clustered-shaft piers, each of these topped by an unusual feature of niches, containing sculptured statues, wrapped round the piers, just under the point where the vaults spring. The nave is 45 metres (148 feet) high. The eastern apsidal end is majestic: built in the 1390s, polygonal in plan, and with the largest east windows in Europe still containing any of their original stained glass. Executed by Filippino da Modena between 1419 and 1430, the glass was reset in the 19th century.

Milan Cathedral covers some 11,700 square metres (14,000 square yards) and was designed to accommodate up to 40,000 people. Although incomplete, in 1577 it was consecrated by Cardinal Archbishop Carlo Borromeo, who was to be canonized in 1610.

Pisa

The cathedral of Santa Maria Maggiore at Pisa has to be considered with its fine separate baptistery just in front of it, and its campanile beside, known to the world as the Leaning Tower of Pisa. This complex of buildings is all part of the ecclesiastical premises of the bishopric, which were begun in the mid-11th century but not finished until the end of the 14th, and there is nothing like it anywhere else in the world. To add emphasis to the unique character of the complex, Pisa was, during the earlier part of the building period, a major school where artists and craftsmen from all over Italy could study and practise and from which they could take the disciplines to other building projects.

The cathedral was begun in the 1080s (the earlier date of 1069 does not seem to be substantiated) by an architect named Busceto,

83

stands on foundations a little over 3 metres (10 feet) deep. The tower began to lean at the end of the 13th century, and the remaining storeys plus belfry (which had not then been completed) were raised in a slightly more vertical line upon the bottom four which were listing. The result is that the tower today actually leans at two perceptibly different angles, and is apparently moving away from the vertical by a minute amount every year.

St Peter's, Rome

The Basilica of St Peter in Rome is not a cathedral, but as it is the largest church in the world it must be included here. And what a masterpiece of architecture it is! Begun by Bramante, continued by Raphael, its major work the creation of Michelangelo, and rounded off, as it were, by Bernini – a unique combination – it houses the tomb of the Big Fisherman, Christ's leading apostle who was put to death in the reign of Emperor Nero.

The spot where St Peter was buried in Rome was marked in 322 by the Emperor Constantine who erected a shrine that was to grow into a substantial basilica within a generation, and become a centre of pilgrimage for hundreds of years. In the 14th and 15th centuries, the old church fell into decay, and in 1450 Pope Nicholas V initiated a scheme to rebuild it. Very little was done, however, and when in 1503 Giuliano della Rovere became Pope Julius II he commissioned Bramante to start afresh and design a new basilica. Bramante produced a perfect symmetrical design on Greek-cross plan, with a central dome and with apsidal ends to each of the four arms. The foundation stone was dedicated in 1506, but by 1514, when Bramante died – Pope Julius had died the previous year – work had only reached the stage of raising the central crossing piers in preparation for the dome. Bramante was succeeded by Raphael, in the years 1514–20, and then by Antonio da Sangallo, but little progress was made.

In 1547, Pope Paul III asked Michelangelo to take on the work, and the great artist-sculptor-architect accepted upon condition

and by the middle of the 12th century much had been done. Then there appear to have been changes in the overall plan, which are not easy to follow, but by the end of the 14th century the plan had taken shape. The cathedral is based on a Roman basilica, with an apsidal east end and round apses at the transept ends. The nave and choir are flanked by double aisles on each side. The tall, robust and yet relatively slim columns, some of them in granite, cylindrical or square, with Corinthian capitals, support side arches with round heads, above which is a twin-arched triforium. Over the central crossing is a cupola, shaped like half an egg and supported on an octagon. There are side chapels in the presbytery and in the transepts. The hemidome over the apsidal east end is decorated with a marvellous mosaic representation of Christ between the Virgin Mary and St John the Baptist.

The cathedral is built of dressed stone and marble, in most parts – particularly the side arches of the naves and the uprights of the triforium – in alternating bands of dark and light, a motif peculiarly Tuscan and which is repeated at Siena and elsewhere. There is a wealth of beautiful decoration and sculpture, among which we must mention the glorious pulpit of Giovanni Pisano, who also worked at Siena.

The exterior of the cathedral is dramatic: the ground storey is covered with blind arcading, with round-headed arches resting on slim columns. Above this are gallery upon gallery of similar or open arcading; at the west front this rises four levels above the ground tier, one gallery straight, the next with sloped edges, the third narrower and straight, and the top in the form of a pediment. The front has three portals with round-headed arches.

The baptistery was begun in 1153–54. It is a cylindrical drum building 35 metres (116 feet) in diameter and about 55 metres (180 feet) tall, with a ribbed hemispherical roof topped by a cone which is in fact the top of an inner shell that pokes out, as at St Paul's in London. The baptistery is decorated outside with similar tiers of blind and open arcading, the second and fourth tiers having pointed, not rounded, arches.

The campanile, or Leaning Tower, is cylindrical, 16 metres (52 feet) across, open-arcaded for six storeys above the blind-arcaded ground storey, with a top belfry of narrower diameter, reaching a total height of 55 metres (180 feet). There is access to the storeys internally by spiral staircases in the wall thickness. The campanile was begun in 1173 and completed in 1350. It is believed to weigh about 14,200 tonnes (14,000 UK tons) and

Right: The crossing at St Peter's, Rome, largely the work of Michelangelo. The baldacchino is by Bernini.

Left: The western front of Pisa Cathedral with its unique arcading. Behind and to the right is the famous Leaning Tower.

Below: The eastern façade of St Peter's, built by Carlo Maderna early in the 17th century, and behind it the supreme architectural achievement of Michelangelo, his great dome.

that he had a free hand – a demand more than justified by his incomparable standing. He was then 72 and devoted the next 17 years until his death to this, his greatest architectural achievement.

Although the supreme artist of his time, he was big enough to admire the work of others, and he accorded the utmost respect to Bramante's plan, modifying it for sheer practical purposes only by strengthening the load-bearing piers for the dome. His basilica was to be vast, but it was constructed in such marvellous proportions that the apsed north, west and south arms of the cross and the barrel-vaulted chapels and aisles, which reached to 30 metres (100 feet), were but a prelude to the tremendous central drum and dome which were later to rise out of them. The drum was finished in his time. Resting upon a ring upon the crown of the main crossing arches and the pendentives between, it has 16 pedimented windows round the circumference. It is 42 metres (138 feet) across, and at its top, where the dome was to sit, it is 73 metres (240 feet) above the ground. When he died, Michelangelo had finished the north, west and south arms and left clear instructions about raising the dome, even making a wooden model to show how it was to be done. The dome was completed by Della Porta and Fontana, who changed Michelangelo's concept, chiefly by altering its curve, so that today with its surmounting lantern and cross it is 138 metres (452 feet) high.

In 1605, Pope Paul V commissioned Carlo Maderna to complete the great basilica. Maderna, though it was 40 years since Michelangelo's death, stood in great awe of him and was anxious to follow his design to its conclusion. But the Pope insisted upon the eastern (nave) arm being extended by three bays,

The superb piazza of Bernini in front of St Peter's, seen from the top of the eastern façade.

partly because Michelangelo's plan did not totally cover the shrine of the old basilica. Maderna was also prevailed upon to put up an eastern façade, fine in itself but sadly obscuring the great dome from people walking up to the portals.

The last great work on St Peter's was the splendid colonnade of the piazza in front of the east end, an elliptical covered portico of four rows of cylindrical columns 18 metres (60 feet) tall and surmounted by a continuous entablature with a procession of sculptured figures above. This was the *tour de force* of Gianlorenzo Bernini (1598–1680), architect to St Peter's from 1629, who also executed a glorious gilded baldacchino, a bronze canopy over the high altar, under the dome.

In a sense, St Peter's represents the apogee of Italian Renaissance art.

Siena

One of the great Italian Gothic cathedrals built under strong Tuscan architectural influence, Siena stands upon a high podium with steps all round. It is an unusual cathedral in that, during the course of its construction history, a second nave was begun at right angles to the first, but was never completed. Instead, the project was abandoned and some of the work pulled down. What remains of the cathedral as a whole is a happy mix of Gothic and Romanesque, with hexagonal base cupola, 16 metres (52 feet) across and nearly 55 metres (180 feet) tall, and striking Gothic western façade. Its pleasing appearance is enhanced by the Tuscan decorative motif of alternating bands of black and white marble on the surfaces.

Siena was begun in the 1220s to replace an earlier church that reached back to the 5th century. Within half a century a marvellous nave with piers of clustered cylindrical columns of alternating black and white marble banding, rising to round-headed arches some 18 metres (60 feet) tall, and with side aisles and a great cupola over the central crossing presented a Romanesque basilica plan. Then the plans

seem to have been changed sharply, for the nave was heightened to take a clerestory topped with a pointed-vault roof. This reduced the prominent role of the cupola. The western façade was started, in typical Gothic fashion, with three fine portals but not quite as deeply recessed as those in some north European cathedrals. The eastern end received a longer choir and presbytery and the transepts were opened up. All this was done by the early 14th century. In the angle between the south side of the nave and the west side of the south transept a splendid campanile was raised, which is immediately distinguished by its alternating bands of black and white marble and its carefully

The interior of Siena Cathedral shows in its highest form the Tuscan style of decorating in marble with alternate light and dark banding. The arresting appearance of the clustered piers is balanced by the round-headed arches springing out of Corinthian capitals.

Overleaf: A marvellous mix of Romanesque and Italian Gothic, the cathedral of Siena is notable for its dark-and-light banding decoration, its 13th-century campanile, and (on the right) the beginning of an extension that was never completed.

graded tiers of lights on the four sides, beginning with a single one at nave-roof level, and rising through two, three, four and five to six at the top. The campanile is topped with a pyramidal roof flanked on the corners with pinnacles.

The western façade had very beautiful sculptural decoration, the lower half the work of Nicola Pisano and his son, Giovanni, of the mid- to late 13th century. Interestingly, the central arch is rounded while the two side arches are pointed, and all three are flanked by carved Tuscan columns. The upper part of the façade was executed a century later and in some specialists' eyes it unbalances the whole.

The interior of Siena is electrifying. The immediate reaction of narrowing one's eyelids to take in the contrasting dark and light of the banding on the piers and walls, at first darkened by the absence of lights in the lower half of the nave, is rapidly altered when one takes in the illumination from the clerestory lights and the huge circular central windows in east and west façades. Then the full glory of the contrasts blends with the deep blue of the painted vaulting, adorned with golden stars, and with the colouring of the stained glass in the rose windows.

Among the exquisite works of art in the cathedral are the universally admired pulpit of

Nicola Pisano, executed in four years (1265–69) in white Carrara marble, the font for the baptistery in the crypt, by Quercia and Donatello in the 1420s, and the high altar of the 1530s by Peruzzi.

St Mark's, Venice

One of the two outstanding examples of Byzantine Christian architecture is St Sophia's Cathedral in Istanbul, which epitomizes the earlier period, from the 4th to the 11th century. The other is St Mark's (San Marco) in Venice, representing the later centuries. It is a magnificent architectural gem, and its position, closing the eastern end of the Piazza di San Marco, at right angles to the Doges' Palace and

Right: The interior of St Mark's Cathedral, Venice, is poorly lit, but nothing diminishes the majesty of the cupolas and their mosaic decoration.

Below: One of the most familiar of all cathedral western fronts, the façade of St Mark's.

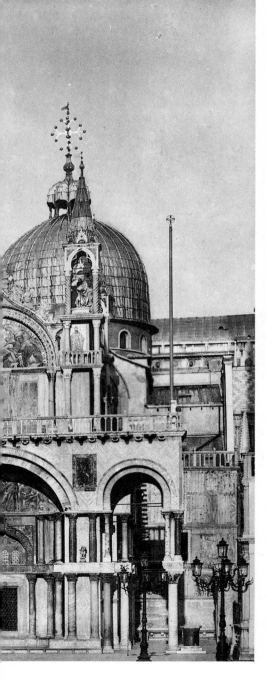

dominated by its 98-metre (323-foot) campanile set slightly to the south-west, prompted Napoleon to describe the piazza as the ballroom of Europe.

The cathedral was a long time in the building. There had been an earlier basilica-type church on the site – and one before that. The second building was badly damaged by fire in the 10th century and in the 1040s work began on the present cathedral which was erected as a chapel for the Doges of Venice, who were the elected chief magistrates of the Venetian Republic. It was built on Greek-cross plan with the arms

of equal length. This is much clearer when you look down upon the cathedral from the campanile, for you can see the five domes over the principal points: the largest, 13 metres (42 feet) across, over the central crossing, and the other four, 10 metres (33 feet) across, over the four arms. The central dome is supported inside, at the crossing, by massive piers, 8.5 metres (28 feet) thick and pierced by arches at ground and gallery levels. These arches support pendentives which carry the dome, as at St Sophia's. The cathedral is 76 metres (250 feet) long and 62 metres (205 feet)

91

Above: The centre portal of the western façade of St Mark's, Venice, which has superb relief decoration in the tympanum. Above are the four bronze horses from Constantinople, in front of the semicircular centre window.

Right: The campanile of the cathedral of St Lawrence in Trogir. Completed in the 16th century, it has fine Venetian Gothic tracery and supports figures of the four evangelists at the corners of the pyramidal roof.

across at the transepts, and the central dome is 28 metres (92 feet) tall inside.

The interior of St Mark's is not as well lit as perhaps is desirable. The 16 windows round each dome base, the wheel window in the south transept, the high windows in the aisles and the small round-headed windows in the apse are all too small, and even the addition of a huge rose window in the west façade in the 15th century, inserted apparently to deal with the light problem, has not solved it. Yet the magnificence of the decoration is dramatic and absorbing. Vaults and domes are covered with masses of glass mosaics in bright colours on a gleaming gold ground, illustrating

in a series of tableaux the principal stories of the Bible, such as the Creation, legends of the saints, and the miracles of Christ.

The most familiar aspect of St Mark's, however, is the celebrated western façade. This is set in two parts. The lower half is a 52-metre (170-foot)-wide narthex with five two-tiered round-headed portals, deeply recessed, with tympana decorated in relief tableaux, the portals flanked by rows of marble columns with capitals, many of which are relics of the earlier (second) church. The top half of the façade is set back, allowing a balustraded platform in front over the lower part of the narthex. This top half consists of a huge circular central window, once decorated with marble tracery. Over the window is a fine ogee arch, and four more slightly smaller ogee arches in line, two on either side, decorated with marble figures, foliage and pinnacles. On the platform stand the four bronze horses that once stood in the hippodrome in Constantinople but were stolen by Venetian crusaders when they sacked Constantinople during the Fourth Crusade, in 1204. The façade is the work of several centuries, from the late 11th to the mid-16th, and displays a mixture of styles among which Gothic is instantly recognizable.

At the south-west corner of the façade stands the lofty campanile built over four centuries (12th–16th) in simple style, square in plan, with flat pilasters and with belfry and pyramidal roof. The campanile collapsed in 1902 but was rebuilt faithfully to the original style soon afterwards.

Yugoslavia

Trogir

About 12 miles (20 kilometres) west of the dramatic remains of the Roman emperor Diocletian's great retirement palace at Spalato (Split) on the Dalmatian coast is Trogir, an ancient town on an island site connected to the mainland by a bridge. Here, at the beginning of the 13th century, on the site of an earlier church that had been sacked by Venetians in the 1170s, was built, in bold Romanesque style, one of

Right: The barrel-vaulted Chapel of St Ivan in the Romanesque cathedral of Trogir was decorated by the native Slav craftsman Aleši. Although in Romanesque style, the chapel was actually added much later, in the 15th century.

Below: This superb entrance portal flanked by two lions supporting columns, at Trogir Cathedral, was the work of Master Radovan, the leading 13th-century Slav artist-craftsman who was trained in Apulia.

the glories of all Dalmatia, Trogir Cathedral. Dedicated to St Lawrence, it is a three-aisle, three-apse basilican structure, with stone vaulting supported on huge rectangular piers. The most splendid feature from its early period is the western entrance, a fine portal flanked by two lions surmounted by statues of Adam and Eve. This is the work of the great sculptor Master Radovan and his assistants and is dated to the 1240s. Supremely confident in his high skills, Radovan autographed the work for posterity. Radovan and his team also produced the glorious reliefs of the Annunciation and the Nativity in the lower part of what

later became the base of a campanile (completed in the 16th century).

The first works at Trogir were finished by about 1250. At about this time, the cathedral miraculously escaped destruction by the Tatars, who had already wrecked many other famous east European cathedrals and churches. The Tatars attempted to besiege the town of Trogir but, strangely, were baulked by its island position, and they left it alone.

In the mid-15th century a fresh burst of building activity began, this time in late Gothic style. The outstanding additions included two cross-vaulted aisles, and the

Chapel of St Ivan, with barrel vaulting. The designer of the chapel was Nicholas of Florence and its principal sculptor and decorator was the great Slav artist Andreja Aleši who also decorated the baptistery of the same period. St Ivan, who had been bishop of Trogir in the 11th century, was also a scientist and something of a miracle-worker. When the Venetians sacked Trogir in the 1170s they tried to remove his corpse as well as the tomb in which it lay, but legend says that the body remained fixed to the floor and only one arm came off, which another legend says was returned mysteriously to Trogir many years later.

Greece

Little Metropole, Athens

Probably the smallest cathedral in the world, the Little Metropole in Athens is claimed to have been founded in 787 by the Byzantine Empress Irene. It is known also as Panayia Gorgoepikoos (The Virgin who grants requests quickly). The cathedral rises from below the level of the adjoining pavement, just to the south of the huge 19th-century Metropolitan Cathedral, which dwarfs it even more.

The Little Metropole is a 12th-century to 13th-century building, rectangular in plan with a rounded apse at the east end. The basic dimensions are only about 12 metres (38 feet) by about 8 metres (25 feet). Over the centre is a cupola, about 3 metres (9 feet) across, on a slender drum pierced by small windows, supported by four piers. The cupola is less than 12 metres (40 feet) tall.

The cathedral is built of white Pentelic marble, faced with decorated Byzantine marble slabs and blocks of various styles, some taken from a number of earlier (6th-century to 9th-century) but ruined churches in Athens, others fragments from much older classical Greek buildings, all together creating a 'dotty historical jumble' of motifs, consisting of zodiac signs, egg-and-dart moulding, mythical animals, and so forth. Over the arch at the west door is an Attic Greek calendar, thought to be about 2nd century A.D.

The smallest cathedral in the world – and one of the oldest – Little Metropole in Athens incorporates stone blocks from the ruins of much earlier buildings.

Cathedrals
of Eastern Europe

Bulgaria

Alexander Nevski Cathedral, Sofia

Behind Sofia's Parliament building over which it towers, Alexander Nevski Cathedral steals the limelight in this interesting capital city of Bulgaria. The cathedral is named after the great Russian hero, Alexander Nevski (1220–63), who was the son of Yaroslav, prince of Novgorod, and who in his time became grand duke of Kiev, Novgorod and Vladimir. The cathedral was built largely between 1904 and 1913 to a design by the Russian architect Pomerantsev, to commemorate the Russians who gave their lives in the liberation of Bulgaria from Ottoman Turkish rule.

The cathedral is an amazing structure. Colossal, it covers 260 square metres (2800 square feet) at ground level, and is over 50 metres (170 feet) tall, rising in clear-cut tiers in diminishing dimensions but still thrusting boldly in profile. Built in cruciform plan, with a five-aisle nave and a huge dome over the central crossing, with subsidiary domes and cupolas, all of them covered with beaten gold leaf which has recently been renovated, it is magnificently Byzantine, inside and out. The

Alexander Nevski Cathedral at Sofia, Bulgaria, built less than a century ago, is strongly influenced by Byzantine and Russian styles.

exterior is built of native
Bulgarian white stone, but for the
inside the architect ordered a
variety of marbles from other
parts of the world, Africa, Brazil
and Italy, and onyx from Mexico.

The interior is sumptuous, and
striking in colour and decorative
effect. Marble columns separate
the narthex from the nave, which
has huge rectilinear piers. There
is a fine central iconostasis
covered with gold leaf. From the
roof hang Byzantine-style
chandeliers, and the walls are
covered with a profusion of
paintings of biblical scenes. Just
as in most ancient Byzantine
churches, the dome at Alexander
Nevski is decorated inside with a
portrait of Christ Pantocrator, in
this case one resembling the
Russian tsar Alexander II. Below
the aisle is a crypt which houses a
remarkable collection of icons and
church regalia, mostly collected
from churches and monasteries in
the Bulgarian countryside.

Bulgaria was once a splendid
empire, forceful, creative,
Christian, then it weakened and
came under Byzantine and later
Turkish rule. Yet Russian
influence has never been far away,
and perhaps the cathedral stands
as a reminder to Bulgaria of who
is boss in Eastern Europe today.

Czechoslovakia

St Vitus's Cathedral, Prague
St Vitus's Cathedral in Prague is
Czechoslovakia's Gothic
masterpiece. Rising majestically
out of the complex of palatial
buildings on Hradcany Hill in the
great Bohemian city, it was built
in the mid-14th century upon the
foundations of two older,
successive Romanesque churches.
The earlier one was founded in
about 930 by Duke Wenceslaus of
Bohemia, the 'Good King
Wenceslaus' of the traditional
Christmas carol, who introduced
Christianity to his country and

Some of the biblical scene paintings that
decorate the interior of Alexander Nevski
Cathedral.

was later canonized as St Wenceslaus. Remains of the old buildings have been preserved in and beside the present cathedral.

The awe-inspiring structure still dominating the skyline in the ancient capital of Bohemia – and now of modern Czechoslovakia – was raised largely in two stages. In the 1340s, Matthias d'Arras, the French architect who had been working for the popes at Avignon, was commissioned by King Charles IV of Bohemia to begin a cruciform-plan cathedral of vast proportions, and the first work, the choir, was built in the French Gothic style, based upon the building work at Narbonne. This choir was to be a hall of fame in which the Bohemian kings were to be crowned and commemorated in portrait busts and recumbent statues. D'Arras died in about 1352 but his influence dominates the lower part of the whole east end of the

cathedral. He was succeeded by Peter Parler, the Swabian master who had been working at Cologne and is described by some architectural historians as the most important architect of the 14th century.

Parler made a tremendous contribution to the appearance of the cathedral, where he completed d'Arras's east end with soaring shafts almost to the full height of the building, and with superb chapels (especially that of St Wenceslaus with its incomparable stellar vault), mingling the pure French Gothic with distinctively English styles, notably with his triforium and its high windows which let in a flood of light. Parler also initiated the fine portrait sculptures, one of which is a self-portrait. The likenesses have been described as unparalleled for their time. He worked at St Vitus's almost until his death at around the turn of the century. His influence in Bohemia was wide-ranging, affecting many buildings of all kinds.

In the 15th century work on the cathedral tailed off as Bohemia was caught up in the challenge to the established Church presented by the Hussites, members of a reforming movement that heralded the great Reformation of the early 16th century. In the late 16th and in the 17th century, construction was resumed but the cathedral was to all intents and purposes completed in the years 1858–1929. The west end of the nave, for example, is less than a century old. Visiting Prague is not easy, even these days, but in the cathedral there vibrates the accumulated creative energy of many centuries of Bohemian history and culture which is not likely to be extinguished under the dead hand of the present satellite regime.

Hungary

Esztergom
The huge, classical, 19th-century cathedral in Hungary's old capital, Esztergom, crowns a hill overlooking the Danube, towering over the ancient city. It is the biggest church in the country, and can be seen from a long distance away, reminding one of the view

The supreme example of Gothic architecture in Czechoslovakia, St Vitus's Cathedral in Prague.

Left: Among the many statues by Peter Parler and his assistants in St Vitus's Cathedral is this one of St Wenceslaus.

The choir and eastern apsidal end, with seven radiating chapels, at St Vitus's Cathedral. The top half is the work of Peter Parler and his assistants.

of Ely Cathedral from Newmarket Heath. Its dome is 100 metres (328 feet) high, while the cathedral itself is 118 metres (387 feet) long and 40 metres (131 feet) wide and can accommodate over 8000 people.

Built between 1820 and about 1870 and resembling St Peter's in Rome in some of its features (though its exterior is almost entirely undecorated), Esztergom was raised round a splendid basilica-type chapel on the Greek-cross plan that had been commissioned in 1507 by Archbishop Tamas Bakocz, the Hungarian primate who nearly became pope, and who was the foremost patron of Renaissance art in 16th-century Hungary. This chapel had risen upon the remains of a much earlier Romanesque church, of the 11th century, when Esztergom was the most important town of the Magyar people. It was destroyed during the appalling raids of the Tatars in the 1240s.

The inside of Esztergom is overpowering. In the 19th-century reconstruction, the Bakocz Chapel was dismantled stone by stone and then re-erected in the body of the new work. The chapel is one of the earliest surviving Renaissance buildings in Hungary, and is of Florentine design, with sculptured ornament executed by Fiorentino. The high altar is approached by 12 steps of red marble, while the sacristy altar is a copy of Titian's *Assumption of the Virgin* and was the work of Grigoletti. The crypt contains the tombs of more than 40 Hungarian notables, including many of the country's archbishops. Among the treasures of the cathedral are the exquisite metalwork motif of the Crucifixion that belonged to Matthias I (king of Hungary 1458–90) and an historic textile panel with gold and silver of 12th-century Byzantine craftsmanship.

Poland

Cracow

No one needs to be reminded today of the crucial importance of religion to the people of Poland. It has been so for more than 1000 years. Perhaps their most treasured religious building – and,

mercifully, one that suffered relatively little during the terrible punishment in the Second World War – is Cracow Cathedral. It was in about 1020 that work began on what was to be the nucleus of a cathedral with a long and important history. St Stanislas, patron saint of Poland, who was bishop of Cracow in the second half of the 11th century, was murdered before the cathedral's high altar by Boleslav II for daring to excommunicate the king for his cruelties and his corrupt private life. St Stanislas is buried at Cracow; so are many other Polish heroes, chief among them the incomparable king John Sobieski, who saved Vienna (and probably Western Europe as well) from the Turks in 1683.

The first cathedral at Cracow was built on the Wawel, the rocky promontory that dominates the city. It was replaced between about 1090 and 1130 by a larger cathedral on cruciform plan, with

A huge Corinthian portico at the western end of Hungary's greatest cathedral, Esztergom, a 19th-century basilican church that incorporates remains of much earlier buildings on the same hill-site.

four towers, which incorporated much of the first church, notably the Romanesque crypt that commemorated St Stanislas, which is today underneath the great nave of the third cathedral on the site. The second cathedral endured severe damage during the Tatar invasions of Polish lands in the 1240s.

The third cathedral, still resplendent today, is in Gothic form, begun in the mid-14th century, and has Renaissance and Baroque additions which enhance rather than spoil its unity. Chief among its Gothic features is the choir with its beautifully carved wooden stalls. In the 1520s,

Sigismund I (king of Poland 1506–48), patron of the Renaissance in Poland and in his grand duchy of Lithuania, commissioned the Florentine Berecci to build and decorate the Sigismund Chapel as a royal mausoleum. This fine chapel on the south side is said to have set the pattern in Poland for Renaissance chapels as centrally planned buildings with dome and lantern. The Sigismund Chapel contains finely sculptured tombs by Berecci and native sculptors working in the cathedral workshops. Paintings and sculptures, including the tomb of King Casimir IV in red marble,

Cracow Cathedral is among the most pleasing ecclesiastical sights in eastern Europe. A church of several styles, it has a completeness that absorbs its long and varied history.

The Romanesque western façade of Romania's Alba Iulia Cathedral, with its Renaissance south-west tower. Note the huge porch over the entrance.

were executed by the German-born Veit Stoss, or Stwosz (1447–1533), who worked in Cracow for many years, and at the end of the 16th century, the Florentine sculptor, Santi Gucci, produced many funerary sculptures, notably the monument to Stephen Bathory, king of Poland from 1575 to 1586. Among the treasures in the cathedral are what is said to be the lance of St Maurice and a relic of St Florian.

Romania

Alba Iulia

Transylvania was for a long time a province of the great medieval kingdom of Hungary, and Alba Iulia, once the Roman colony of Apulum, became an important city within the region as early as

the 10th century. A church of Lombard-German design was built there, on basilican plan, and this became a cathedral when Ladislaus I (king of Hungary 1077–95) founded the bishopric of Alba Iulia. The first work was finished early in the 13th century. Then, in 1241–42, Transylvania was engulfed by the Tatar invasions of south-east Europe, and the cathedral, along with so many other buildings, was sacked.

In the years from 1250 to about 1300, Alba Iulia Cathedral was rebuilt, this time in Romanesque style upon the original basilican plan, with a nave and two aisles, all with apses, and a transept which later received a tower. It was supervised to begin with by a French architect, who introduced cross vaulting in the early Gothic manner. Fine bas-reliefs were

sculpted in the central apse. Work also began on the western façade, which was later to have a high Gothic open-vaulted porch flanked by two towers. The porch was topped with a triangular pediment with four Baroque-style statues in the early 18th century. One of the towers, completed by Italian craftsmen in the early 17th century, is in several stages, like a campanile.

Turkey

St Sophia's, Istanbul

For nearly 1000 years the cathedral of St Sophia (Hagia Sophia) at Istanbul (known as Constantinople until 1930) was Christendom's greatest church. Then, in 1453, it was taken over by the Muslim Turks and turned into a mosque. Today much of its original decoration, particularly its fine mosaics, which had been covered for centuries with plaster, is now being revealed in all its pristine glory.

St Sophia's is a building of superlatives. It was designed inside a month. It was built inside six years (532–537) to a plan by two leading Greek architects, Anthemius of Tralles and Isodorus of Miletus, commissioned by Justinian I (Byzantine emperor 527–565) who spared no expense. Over 10,000 craftsmen and labourers were employed more or less the whole time, and when it was complete, barring some of the interior decoration, Justinian exclaimed: 'Solomon, I have outdone thee!'

The cathedral is built of brick and stone. It was erected on the site of two earlier succeeding churches and its plan is almost square. The foundations are said to have been placed on 6 metres (20 feet) of concrete. Its central feature is its huge, shallow-arced dome, 33 metres (107 feet) across and nearly 55 metres (180 feet) from the ground. It is supported on huge triangular pendentives stemming from four semicircular arches, set on four stone piers over the central area inside, with semidomes at east and west partially supporting the structure by containing the thrust and counterthrust within. The

Left: Under the vast dome of the cathedral of St Sophia in Istanbul.

Below: With minarets added by Ottoman sultans, the cathedral of St Sophia (Hagia Sophia) at Istanbul (once Constantinople) in Turkey was the supreme ecclesiastical building of the Byzantines. It was built in the very short time of six years.

construction produced a huge oval nave, 33 metres (107 feet) wide and 69 metres (225 feet) long, which is magnificently lit by the 40 small arched windows piercing the lower part of the dome and by virtue of the vast interior height. The dome was built of brick with mortar joints. It was seriously endangered after an earthquake in the 14th century and massive buttresses were erected against north and south sides of the complex. The piers, walls and arches were faced with marble of a variety of shades, white, blue, green, red and black. The columns were of solid coloured marble and the floors were of coloured mosaic, some with gilded background.

There is an irony about the two occasions on which the cathedral was captured during assaults on Constantinople. In 1202, Pope Innocent III organized the Fourth Crusade, but long before the crusaders, this time mainly French and Venetian soldiery, had reached their goal of the Holy Land, in 1204, they changed direction and headed for Constantinople instead, to prosecute a commercial and religious dispute with the Byzantine Empire. They found the city poorly defended and they broke in and sacked it. The great

Left: Wall paintings inside the huge cathedral of St Sophia at Kiev, in the U.S.S.R.

cathedral was not spared: terrible things were done there. Mosaics were ripped up, icons smashed, gold and silver wall fittings wrenched away. Tombs were desecrated and works of art looted and taken to the West. It was one of the most disgraceful episodes in the history of Christendom. In pleasing contrast, when the Muslim Sultan Mohammed II besieged and took Constantinople in 1453, he ordered that the cathedral was to be spared. When he was told of a Turkish soldier being caught tearing up a mosaic, he had him flogged. It was Mohammed's ambition to set up a throne in the great building and then to proclaim it as a mosque for Islam.

U.S.S.R.

St Sophia's, Kiev

St Sophia's in Kiev is probably the oldest cathedral in all Russia. It is also one of the largest. Built on an almost square plan, it has been so altered or added to that

The 21-domed cathedral of St Sophia in Kiev, reconstructed in the 18th century, is now a museum. It was begun almost 950 years ago.

These mosaic figures of saints and Church fathers, in the eastern apse of St Sophia's Cathedral, Kiev, were executed in the early 11th century.

its original character is almost lost. But with its 21 domes (some of them medieval, some of them 18th-century Russian Baroque), its nine aisles (each with semicylindrical apses), its profusion of flying buttresses which support a vast encircling one-storey gallery, and its massive cruciform piers, it is still an astonishing structure, surrounded now by walls. These are dominated by a golden cupola-topped campanile acting as an entrance gate, some 78 metres (256 feet) tall and visible for many miles across the steppe.

St Sophia's was begun in the 1020s by Yaroslav the Wise, grand prince of Kiev, who was son of St Vladimir. It was part of a building programme to make Kiev comparable with – if possible superior to – Constantinople. In its first form it was a huge cruciform church with five aisles, crowned with 13 domes (the central dome about 8 metres (25 feet) across) to represent Christ and his 12 disciples. The north, west and south sides of the inside were surrounded by a

single-storey gallery. Yaroslav dedicated the cathedral in about 1037, intending it to be the burial place for the princes of Kiev. In the 12th century the cathedral was extended: four more aisles were added and the gallery was remodelled and enlarged, supported by flying buttresses. Two towers and eight more domes were erected.

The interior of St Sophia's was decorated with mosaics and frescoes of the highest quality, remarkable for their arresting colours. Some of them were produced in the first building phases of the 11th century, most notably the mosaic in the central dome which is of Christ Pantocrator (a predominating Byzantine style) surrounded by a circle of archangels, and the figures of the saints and fathers of the Greek Church in the central apse. The earlier frescoes are in fragmentary condition. Among the monuments is the marble tomb of Prince Yaroslav who is buried there.

In 1240 the Mongols stormed, sacked and occupied Kiev, leaving it like a city after an air raid. St Sophia's was damaged and left to deteriorate for centuries. Then, in the 18th century, it was extensively restored and modified. The original façades had been unadorned, but in the Baroque age, when it was fashionable to decorate exteriors elaborately, St Sophia's received a new look of Ukrainian Baroque style, with decorated walls, rich new domes, ornamented portals and windows. In the 1740s work began on the campanile which rose through four storeys to a height of 78 metres (256 feet).

Today, St Sophia's is a museum. One among the vast number of ancient treasures surviving is an impressive mosaic of the Communion of the Apostles, executed in about 1110 for the nearby monastery of St Michael by Greek mosaic masters working in the cathedral with the assistance of local craftsmen. The mosaic was later moved into the cathedral.

St Isaac's, Leningrad
The huge, monumental, domed 19th-century cathedral of St Isaac

in Leningrad, the biggest church in northern Russia, was largely the work of a French architect. Yet it is very Russian, mixed with distinctive classical features. It stands upon the beginnings of a cathedral designed by the Italian architect Rinaldi who was invited to work in Leningrad (or St Petersburg as it was then known) in the 1760s by Catherine the Great. His cathedral was not finished. Then, in 1816, invitations to produce designs for a new cathedral on the site were opened to architects in Europe, and in 1817, 30-year-old Ricard de Montferrand, from France, won the competition. For the rest of his life he supervised the erection of an astonishing structure which he had planned in Imperial Russian style. It is built of marble and granite, some of the latter from Finland, and it is a dominating building even in Leningrad which possesses several of the finest and most interesting structures in Europe.

St Isaac's is based on the Greek-cross plan and is 111 metres (365) feet long and 98 metres (320 feet) wide. It has a huge central gilded dome, over 100 metres (330 feet) tall, on a colonnaded drum, surrounded by smaller cupolas. The top can be reached by staircases with a total of 562 steps. From the ceiling is suspended a huge pendulum

Leningrad has five cathedrals, but the greatest is St Isaac's, built of granite and marble.

Part of the enormous iconostasis at St Isaac's Cathedral, Leningrad, which is 69 metres (225 feet) wide.

weighing over 50 kilograms (110 pounds), designed by the horologist Foucault. The pendulum demonstrates the rotation of the earth on its axis.

Inside, the dominant feature beneath the dome and the high vaulting is the iconostasis, which is of gilded marble, lapis lazuli and malachite. It is 69 metres (225 feet) long and has 33 mosaic icons. The walls are heavily ornamented with polychrome marble slabs, hung with numerous paintings by Russian and other artists.

The outside has two façades, northern and southern, which are imitations of the famous Pantheon in Rome. There are 16 monolith columns of granite over 15 metres (50 feet) tall, with bronze bases and capitals, at each entrance.

The columns support a pediment decorated with bronze relief sculptures. The entrance doors are made of beaten bronze, designed by Vitali, and each of them weighs more than 10 tonnes (10 UK tons).

St Basil the Blessed, Moscow
Proud as a bastion of Christianity despite its secular use as a museum, and seeming to defy the godless architecture of the monolithic Kremlin buildings and the Lenin Mausoleum nearby in Moscow's Red Square, stands the gay, ornate, bizarre nine-towered cathedral of St Basil. Begun in the 1550s by the great Russian Tsar Ivan IV (the Terrible) to commemorate his victory over the Tatar Mongols at Kazan in 1552, and taking over a century to

Looking up into the huge drum that supports the dome of St Isaac's Cathedral in Leningrad.

finish, St Basil's represents the apogee of the Russian-Byzantine style, essentially a national form of architecture. In its fantastic form the cathedral combines Byzantine plan, mosaic and fresco decoration inside, with a fresh Western Renaissance exterior of angular pediments, rosettes, panels, machicolations, and round-headed and pointed arches, mingled happily if eccentrically with native Russian onion-capped towers, *kokoshniki* and bright-hued brick façades.

Designed by two leading Russian architects, Barma and Postnik, its immediately chaotic appearance belies its essential harmony. There was a setback when the cathedral was pillaged by Polish forces in 1611, and it was not completed until the 1670s.

The plan is a symmetrical conglomerate of polygonal towers, or towerlike chapels as separate but grouped units, eight of them positioned almost equidistantly round a ninth, larger central octagon. The eight chapels are topped with onion caps, whose surfaces are treated differently, some diamond-faceted, some ribbed, some tiled, but all decorated in brilliant colours. Over the central tower is a tall, octagonal steeple, instead of a traditional dome, rising to a *shater* (an octagonal tent roof) with a small onion cap at the top which is about 33 metres (107 feet) tall. Interestingly, the design of St Basil's was influenced by the then flourishing and typically Russian wood-dominated architecture which was employed for palaces

Below the drums supporting the onion-topped domes of St Basil's Cathedral in Moscow are some fine examples of *kokoshniki* (rows of arches).

damage again during the Second World War, but this was repaired in the 1950s.

Cathedral of the Assumption, Vladimir

Clean, white in its snowy sandstone material, the Cathedral of the Assumption stands inside the citadel on the hill at Vladimir, overlooking the Klyazma river. Topped by five domes, the cathedral was begun in the 1150s by Andrei Bogolyubski, grand prince of Vladimir-Suzdal and a direct descendant of St Vladimir, founder of Russian Christianity.

Prince Andrei, a keen builder and patron of art, and fond of decorative work, sponsored many splendid buildings. His white cathedral was rectangular, three-aisled, and surmounted with a single central dome supported on pendentives in the manner of the great dome of St Sophia's in Istanbul. He died in 1175. Eight years later, the cathedral was severely damaged in a fire, but this gave his brother, Vsevolod III, a marvellous opportunity to rebuild the cathedral on a much grander scale. He erected buildings on all sides, adding two more aisles to the original three and giving it four more domes, one over each of the angles.

Vsevolod shared his brother's enthusiasm for decoration inside and outside. The white glow of the façades was sharpened by contrasting gilded columns and ornamental motifs painted in fresco in the niches. Between the columns were fresco-painted portraits of saints or elaborately sculptured stone scenes with human and animal figures. The interior was likewise decorated with frescoes, but only fragments of those of Vsevolod's time remain.

In 1238, Vladimir, which had become the capital of Russia in the 1160s, was savagely assaulted by the Mongols and most of its great buildings were looted and damaged, including the cathedral and a second cathedral of St Dimitri, built nearby by Vsevolod in the 1190s. For a long time the whole of Russia languished under Mongol dominion, but in the late 14th century there was a revival of building and art. Andrei

and peasants' cottages alike.

During Napoleon's invasion of Russia in 1812, the French army reached Moscow only to find it deserted. St Basil's was desecrated by the French cavalry who used it as a stable for their horses. When the emperor decided to evacuate Moscow, he gave the order to one of his generals to destroy it, an order which most fortunately was not carried out. Yet some damage must have been done, for in the period 1839–45, major restorations were necessary. St Basil's suffered

Rublev (*c.* 1365–*c.* 1430), probably the greatest religious painter in the history of Russian art, was commissioned to restore decoration and add new work in the cathedral, over the years 1408–12. Some of this has survived, notably his marvellous *Apostles and Angels, Christ among the Seraphim,* and many figures of prophets.

The Cathedral of the Assumption numbered among its many treasures the most sacred of all Russian icons, called the Virgin of Vladimir, which had been painted in Constantinople in about 1125. This beautiful portrait of Mary, the mother of Christ, with her son, became a major influence upon the native Russian tradition of icon art, and was 'the inspiration for hundreds of attempts to portray the Virgin and Child with a comparable rendering of tenderness'. At the end of the 14th century it was moved to Moscow.

The 12th-century Cathedral of the Assumption at Vladimir from the northeast.

Cathedrals of the U.S.A.

St John the Divine, New York
The Episcopal cathedral of St John the Divine in New York has been claimed as the largest Gothic cathedral in the world. It may well be so when it is completed. Even now it is massive, full of superlatives, and appropriate for one of the greatest cities on earth.

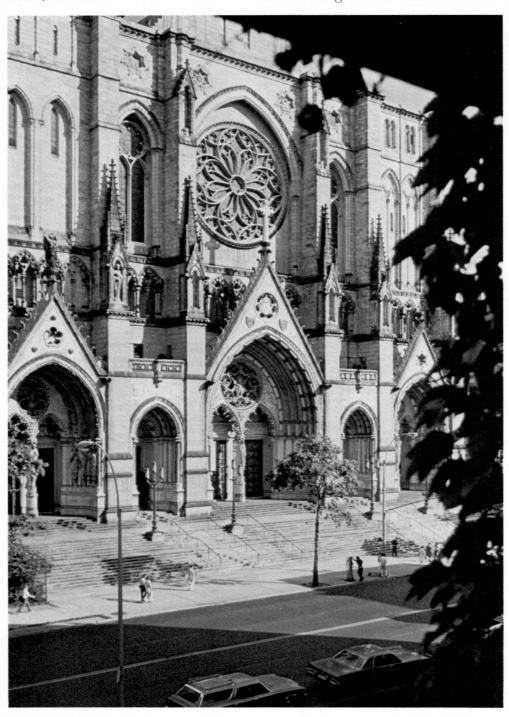

The Gothic-style western façade of the Protestant Cathedral of St John the Divine, New York.

The idea of a huge cathedral in New York was the conception of Bishop Horatio Potter in the 1870s. In 1892 his nephew Henry bought the land for it and the foundation stone was laid on 27 December. The architects Henis and La Farge conceived a European Romanesque structure, and the first works, the narthex and the choir, reflected this style. But by 1910, as further work was carried out, it began to assume Gothic features, and from that time the cathedral was to be built in European Gothic, with some relationship with Notre-Dame in Paris. During the First World War the choir, crossing and sanctuary were finished. The sanctuary is half surrounded by a fine arc of columns of granite, about 17 metres (55 feet) high, which fits well with its Romanesque part. Work then tailed off, but in the 1920s a fund was opened and about $15 million was collected, enabling the great nave to be begun. By the time it was complete, in 1939, there were five naves 76 metres (250 feet) long and spreading over 46 metres (150 feet), with arches reaching to a height of 38 metres (125 feet). The full length of the cathedral is 183 metres (601 feet).

The cathedral is still unfinished, and about a quarter remains to be done, chiefly the completion of two towers on the western front, the north and south transepts and the central tower. The western front is just over 60 metres (200 feet) wide. Its towers will eventually rise to 80 metres (265 feet). There are five portals which line up with the five naves, but they have not yet been completed. The centre portal has bronze doors made by the same Parisian firm that made the Statue of Liberty. The great rose window above is nearly 12 metres (40 feet) across and is said to be glazed with 10,000 pieces of stained

glass. The central tower will be crowned with a spire reaching to 137 metres (450 feet). One of the cathedral's many unusual features is a biblical garden in which the trees are exclusively those species mentioned in the Bible.

Inside the cathedral there is a model of what it will eventually be like when all the work is done. The story of the building of St John the Divine over the past 90 years is a remarkably cogent 'carbon copy' of how cathedrals were built in earlier times, work proceeding in fits and starts, interrupted by funds running out, followed by appeals and then renewed works, with changes in design and so forth.

St Patrick's, New York

This is the principal Roman Catholic cathedral in the United States, and more people of all faiths are said to visit it than any other in the country. Dwarfed as it is by the gigantic Rockefeller Center with its skyscraper, St Patrick's is nonetheless a splendid and lofty structure well fitted to be the church of the Roman Catholic archbishopric of New York.

The conception of the cathedral was announced in 1850 when the site was chosen by the then bishop, on the edge of the growing city. Few people appreciated, however, that New York would expand northwards, and there was considerable grumbling that the new centre of Catholicism would be so inaccessible. The foundations were nonetheless laid and a great Gothic cathedral based to some extent on the design of Cologne began to go up,

The superb Romanesque-style choir and apsidal end of the world's biggest cathedral, St John the Divine, in New York, built in the first years of the present century.

Above: The vista towards the apsidal end in the Cathedral of St Peter and St Paul in Washington is such as one would meet in the greatest medieval Gothic cathedrals of Europe.

Left: The 19th-century cathedral of St Patrick in New York, built as a faithful copy of medieval Gothic.

and by 1888, the best part of the work was done. By that time, expansion of New York had indeed moved northwards and had absorbed the cathedral. Today, standing on Fifth Avenue, it is of course right in the heart of this astonishing city.

Built on cruciform plan, largely of white marble and stone, St Patrick's is 123 metres (405 feet) long. Its nave, a beautiful construction, is 38 metres (125 feet) across and has tall cross-ribbed Gothic arches which are supported upon massive 11-metre (35-foot) marble piers, giving a vault height of 34 metres (112 feet). The east end terminates in a fine Lady Chapel, added in 1903–07, which is glazed with exquisite stained glass, much of it intense blue and made specially at Chartres. In all there are 70 stained-glass windows.

The western façade, which fronts on to Fifth Avenue, has three portals, the centre one of which is topped by a tall, sharp triangular arch. The doors of this portal are of finely sculptured bronze. Above the portals is a rose window 8 metres (26 feet) in diameter. Flanking the western façade are two richly carved Gothic towers reaching to 101 metres (332 feet). The cathedral was finished in 1910 and consecrated a year later.

Washington

The Cathedral of St Peter and St Paul, also known as Washington Cathedral, is not yet completed. But three-quarters has been built, in Gothic style, and one can see that it is English-looking. Viewed from the south-east, with its east end, its south transept and its 90-metre (300-foot)-tall tower over the central crossing, the cathedral reminds one of Worcester looked at from the same vantage point. As one of the major churches of so large and important a nation, Washington Cathedral is of course bigger than Worcester – indeed, when finished it will be 160 metres (525 feet) long and among the 10 largest ecclesiastical buildings in the world. The transepts, already completed, span 84 metres (275 feet), and the nave height is 30 metres (100 feet).

Washington Cathedral stands upon a marvellously dominating site on Mount St Alban, 120 metres (400 feet) over the Potomac river, in the north-west of the nation's capital. The site was chosen in 1898 and work began in 1907 to a design by G. F. Bodley (1827–1907), the well-known English architect, famous as an exponent of High Gothic style. The foundation stone was brought from a quarry near Bethlehem.

Designed on cruciform plan, the early works were slow. Among the first buildings were the eastern octagonal apsidal end with its sanctuary, surrounded by radiating chapels in the French Gothic manner. These were built over the eastern crypt, the easternmost structure in which is the Bethlehem Chapel, the very first completed work (1908–12). The choir, of five bays, was finished in 1932. Four years later, the Children's Chapel, erected on the south side near the south transept, was completed and it is one of only two such chapels in the world specially designed for children. It has a sensitive statue of Christ with his arms wide open as if saying 'Suffer the little children to come unto me', and the carving on the mouldings incorporates motifs which are designed to delight children, such as squirrels.

Left: The Scientists and Technicians Window in Washington Cathedral. Also known as the Space Window, it incorporates, in the centre of the red orb, a sliver of moon rock presented by Apollo 11's crew.

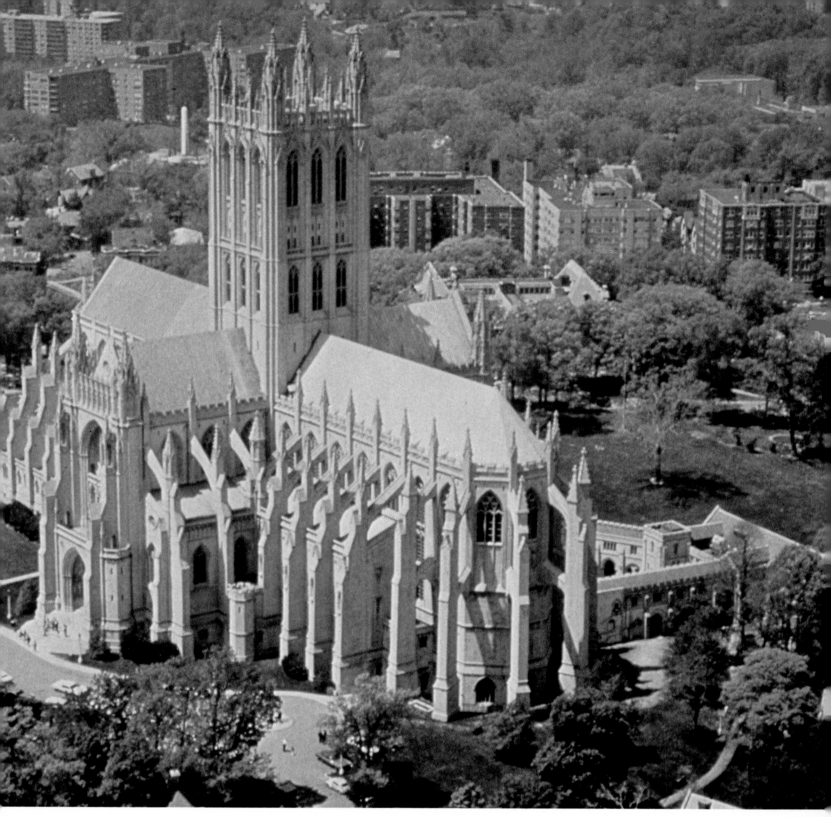

Under the central crossing is a crypt chapel dedicated to St Joseph of Arimathea, built in late 12th-century style, whose walls are formed by four gigantic corner piers about 8 metres (26 feet) across, which are the bases for the piers that rise through the ceiling into the cathedral to support the central tower. This tower is known as the Gloria in Excelsis, and was started in 1961. The tower holds a 53-bell carillon. The nave, which is flanked by double aisles on each side, with triforium and clerestory, is nine-bayed. The western front has a deeply recessed porch and when completed with its two western towers (scheduled to reach 70 metres (230 feet)) will resemble the west end of Canterbury.

Grace Cathedral, San Francisco

Grace is a modern Gothic-style cathedral of major proportions, worthy of comparison with the medieval Gothic masterpieces on which it is modelled. About 98 metres (320 feet) long and 50 metres (165 feet) wide at the transepts, with a central spire

Though not yet complete, the huge Cathedral of St Peter and St Paul, Washington, is a splendid reproduction of English Gothic, with a more French Gothic apsidal end.

The eastern façade of Grace Cathedral, San Francisco, recalls the western façades of the Ile de France Gothic cathedrals. The whole church is built of structural steel and concrete, yet lacks little of the medieval feel.

rising to a cross at 80 metres (265 feet), two façade towers reaching 52 metres (170 feet) and a fine nave 28 metres (92 feet) tall, it is remarkable for having been begun and completed within a period of only 36 years, an achievement that even the builders of Amiens or Salisbury would have envied. Grace stands on Nob Hill, a site envisaged by the bishop of San Francisco soon after the terrible earthquake and consequent fire that destroyed so much of this western seaboard metropolis in 1906. A foundation stone was laid in 1910 but nothing else was done until 1928.

Grace is built on cruciform plan. The first buildings to go up were the chancel, an interesting Chapel of Grace upon the south side of the chancel and the transepts. The nave was begun at the central crossing end. Then the work came to an abrupt stop because of the great Wall Street Crash, and the incompleted nave was boarded up. Enough had been built, however, for it to be used. In 1938, a marvellous carillon of 44 bells was presented to Grace by a Cornish-born millionaire who also donated the funds to build the north tower on the east façade in which the bells would eventually ring out their peals.

The last stages of the work were carried out with tremendous verve and speed, in the years 1956–64, when the central tower was finished and its spire lifted into place by crane, the last three bays of the nave completed and the south tower on the façade built. On 20 November 1964 San Francisco's great cathedral was consecrated.

Grace is constructed largely of structural steel and concrete: it has to be because of the city's liability to earth tremors. This has meant that it does not have all the traditional features of a Gothic cathedral that it strives to imitate. There is no triforium, flying buttresses are not required, and curved parts such as apse ends had to be made polygonally. Where there is moulding and ornament, it has usually been made by special moulds into which concrete was poured. To give the concrete colour, stones of many shades were included in the aggregate. Yet it is all so well done that one might well be looking at a medieval stone structure.

The cathedral has modern stained glass which future ages will undoubtedly compare favourably with medieval work. And the decoration inside is superb. The rose window in the east end, just above the main portal, is in faceted glass and was made in Chartres. The stained glass filling the cathedral's 60-odd tall windows transports the visitor effortlessly back to the Middle Ages.

The entrance to St Mary's Cathedral of the Assumption, San Francisco. This building replaced the old cathedral destroyed by fire in 1962 and witnessed the celebration of its first Mass in 1970. Architecturally dramatic and ultra-modern, it has four massive concrete pylons which support a tower nearly 60 metres (200 feet) high which is topped by a 15-metre (50-foot) crucifix.

Cathedrals of Central and South America

Mexico

Mexico Cathedral

Probably the supreme architectural achievement of the Spanish during their occupation of both central and south America, Mexico Cathedral, an exciting mix of Spanish Renaissance, Baroque and Classical, and even Gothic elements, and built of limestone and volcanic stone, with marble embellishments, is the largest church in Mexico. Its magnificent western façade, Baroque with classical impositions, fronts on to the Plaza de Armas in the city centre.

The cathedral was begun in 1573 upon the site of an earlier, smaller church put up by the first Spaniards in the 1520s, which itself was superimposed upon the remains of an Aztec temple. The foundation stone was laid by the Spanish viceroy, de Almanza, on behalf of Philip II of Spain who was anxious to create a substantial and beautiful centre of Spanish Christian worship in the New World.

As it turned out, Mexico Cathedral was nearly 250 years in the building. The structure is vast, 117 metres (385 feet) long and 54 metres (177 feet) wide. Built in Latin-cross form with a dome over the central crossing, the interior is lofty and awe-inspiring, with its rows of clustered fluted columns along the sides of the nave. The choir is divided from the main part of the cathedral by screens of exquisite ironwork of the 18th century, and wrought-iron screens also fence off a variety of chapels leading off the aisles. Behind the high altar at the east end of the nave is the Chapel of the Kings, which is graced by a magnificent Churrigueresque gilded and carved wood altarpiece, and in which there are paintings by Juárez. The sacristy is notable for its Gothic ribbed vaults. The crypt contains the tombs of many Mexican archbishops.

The highlight of the exterior is the splendid façade of three Baroque portals, flanked by columns, and the crowning piece, neo-classical with balustrades on top. At each end of the façade is a 71-metre (232-foot)-tall tower topped by a bell-shaped cupola. Over the central crossing is a great dome and lantern.

Right: The eastern end of Mexico Cathedral, with its tall, fluted-shaft piers supporting Classical vaulting, is marvellously lit through spacious windows.

Below: The western façade of the Spanish Baroque cathedral in Mexico City towers over the huge Plaza de Armas in the city centre.

Mexico Cathedral has a rich store of treasures, including paintings by Murillo, Correa and Villapando, and silver and gold ornaments and church plate said to be worth millions of dollars.

Brazil

Brasília

One of the more interesting cathedrals built in the modern idiom is the cathedral at Brasília, the new capital city of Brazil. The city is about 1100 metres (3500 feet) above sea level, nearly 750 miles (1200 kilometres) north-west (by road) from Rio de Janeiro, on the central plateau of Brazil, where the sunlight is intense. The cathedral is the work of Brazil's leading native architect Oscar Niemeyer, principal designer of the city, and it was begun in 1959. It is on the north side of the city and is the cathedral of a new archbishopric.

The cathedral is circular in plan, and the nave, with the high altar and other features, is laid out on a floor some 3 metres (10 feet) below ground level. This is approached by means of slightly inclined underground walkways. The floor is encircled by a massive ring of concrete, 60 metres (200 feet) in diameter and about 3 metres (10 feet) high, which is the wall of the nave. Out of this rise 16 equidistantly placed concrete ribs, or buttresses, beginning at very acute angles, then curving sickle-shaped as they sweep inwards to cluster together in the centre to form a sheaf, and finally curving upwards and outwards to a height of about 31 metres (102 feet). This 'thorny corona' at the top holds a concrete slab, the roof, which is about 12 metres (40 feet) across. The spaces between the buttresses are filled with glazed grids of thin ironwork which serve to diffuse

Left: The altarpiece of the Chapel of the Kings, at Mexico Cathedral, is in Churrigueresque style.

Below: Inside Brasília's ultra-modern interdenominational cathedral. The floor is about 3 metres (10 feet) below ground level and 16 concrete ribs rise from around it to support a ceiling from which sculptures of angels are suspended.

the intense sunlight outside and to
spread it warmly and comfortably
round the nave below. The
surfaces of the buttresses are light-
coloured to deflect sunlight.
Suspended from the ceiling are
fine sculptures of angels, and out
of the top of the roof slab projects
a gilded cross.

The cathedral endured the
hiccoughs in its building progress
that have been common to all
cathedrals, but it was finished in
1980. It stands inside a
rectangular enclosure bounded on
three sides by ranges of low-level
buildings (not yet completed)
which provide offices, living
quarters, museum, chapels and so
forth.

Peru

Cuzco

The fine Spanish Renaissance
cathedral at Cuzco is among the
highest in the world, for it stands
dominating the ancient capital of
the Incas, some 3360 metres
(11,000 feet) above sea level. After
they had crushed the Inca empire
in the 1530s, the Spanish
conquistadores began to erect
their own buildings on Inca ruins.
We do not know when the
cathedral was started, but some
work had been carried out before
a shattering earthquake rocked
Cuzco in 1650. After the dust had
settled, as it were, construction
was resumed, and a church of

Above: Statues of the Apostles stand
guard beside the 'thorny corona' at the
top of Oscar Niemeyer's remarkable
modern cathedral at Brasília, Brazil's
new capital city.

Above: The formidable western façade of Cuzco Cathedral in Peru.

Left: The striking cone-shaped exterior of Rio de Janeiro's New Cathedral, which was dedicated in 1976. Four enormous stained-glass windows are an exciting feature of the interior.

simple plan based upon a design by Veramendi was erected by Correa and Becerra (who had built the cathedral at Lima, some 350 miles (550 kilometres) northwest). The church was raised upon the remains of an ancient palace and temple of the Inca emperor Viracocha.

Cuzco Cathedral is in the Plaza de Armas, on to which its western façade abuts. This façade has a squat, square bell tower with cupola on each end, well spaced out with a Baroque portal in the centre, whose heavy doors are studded with bronze nails. The portal has unusual wood ornament in a markedly Inca style, explained by the fact that the façade was built largely with the help of many Peruvian Indians, some of whom were, no doubt, descendants of the Inca people. The cathedral is three-aisled, with cross vaulting, and has a splendid choir with Baroque stalls, and a sacristy with a reredos bearing a Christ that is attributed to Van Dyck, the Flemish painter better known for portraits of Charles I of England, Scotland and Ireland and his family.

The cathedral is built of evenly cut brown stone blocks, some of them reused stones from the old Inca structure, some cut from the same supply quarries, producing a pleasing blend. There is severe restraint in the ornamentation, unlike Spanish cathedrals of the same period built in Mexico, but the interior has a considerable display of pictures.

Some time after the completion of the main work, two smaller churches were grafted on to its north and south sides, and the three are all connected.

Lima Cathedral, in Peru's capital, was begun in the 16th century. It was consecrated in 1625 but the two towers were not finished until the late 1640s. The cathedral was twice damaged in earthquakes, in 1687 and 1746, and was then restored. This is the western front.

Glossary

Aisle A passageway flanked by a wall on one side and columns on the other, or by columns on both sides.

Ambulatory A walkway flanked by columns round the east end of a church, behind the high altar.

Apse A rounded, polygonal or rectangular end or projection, usually, though not only, at the east end of a cathedral. An apse generally has a vaulted roof.

Arcade A row of arches, open or closed, supported on columns or piers. An arcade may form the lower part of a wall, along a nave for example.

Arches There are several types including:
Rounded or round-headed: semicircular.
Pointed: the two curved sides meeting at a point.
Ogee: double curved, the line of which is concave, then convex.

Arrow loop A long, narrow vertical opening in a wall.

Baldacchino A canopied structure, usually of marble or stone, erected over an altar.

Balustrade Railing or fence composed of rows of upright members (balusters) supporting a handrail or parapet coping, made of wood, iron or stone.

Baptistery Chapel or space in a cathedral set aside for baptisms, containing a font. The baptistery is a separate building at some cathedrals (such as Pisa and Florence).

Baroque From the Portuguese *barrocco*, an irregularly shaped pearl, 'Baroque' is a term describing a style of architecture and decoration using strong curves, diagonals, with emphasis produced by strong contrasts of dark and light.

Barrel vault See **Vault**.

Basilica From the Greek word for a king, 'basilica' means 'king's throne room'. In Roman times, a rectangular hall of justice or administration, with rounded apse end where the tribunal sat. Early Christians adapted the hall, giving it a nave with aisles and an entrance chamber (narthex, q.v.).

Bas-relief Shallow sculpture or carving on a background, less than the true depth, in stone or metal.

Bay Compartment of a nave bounded by columns or piers and composed of three levels, arcade, triforium and clerestory.

Belfry A bell tower.

Blind arcade Row of arched recesses in a wall.

Buttress A vertical mass of brick or masonry built against a wall to strengthen it or to support a heavy roof truss or vault.

Campanile A cathedral's bell tower that is separated from the main building.

Capital The crowning piece of a column or pilaster.

Carillon A set of bells.

Cartouche A panel ornamented at the edges with inward curving scrolls, the panel generally bearing an inscription or heraldic device.

Chancel The sacred area of the cathedral, generally the east end, including the choir and the high altar. The chancel is sometimes called the choir. Other names used are 'sanctuary' or 'presbytery'. The term means 'cancelling out', or shutting off from the rest of the cathedral, hence its separation from the rest by a screen or pulpitum (q.v.).

Chapter house The office and meeting room of a chapter, the governing body of a cathedral.

Chevet French term for the rounded apsidal end of a cathedral where it includes an ambulatory with an arc of chapels (radiating chapels). It is a feature of French Gothic style.

Chevron Zigzag, or inverted 'V'-shaped, a type of ornamental moulding, usually round an arch. It is typical of Romanesque decoration.

Choir Strictly speaking, it is the area east of the screen or pulpitum and west of the presbytery, where the choir stalls are sited. The term 'choir' is sometimes used loosely to embrace the east end. Some choirs extend west into the crossing, one or two even into the nave.

Churrigueresque A Spanish style of Baroque, influenced by native styles of Central and South America, it was introduced by José Churriguera (1650–1725), the Salamanca architect, and his family.

Classical style In the styles of the architecture of ancient Greece and Rome.

Clerestory The upper part of the nave, choir and transept walls, below the roof levels and above the roof of the aisle, which is pierced by windows. Not all cathedrals have a clerestory.

Clustered column A column that appears as one member but which is a bunch of several shafts.

Corbel A block of stone or wood projecting from a wall specifically to support a beam or vault, or a statue. Corbels were usually decorated with sculpture or carving.

Corona A circular chandelier hung from the roof of a church.

Crossing In a cruciform church, the space where the transepts intersect with the eastern and western arms, over which is usually raised a tower or dome.

Cruciform Church plan based on a cross.

Cupola A word variously used to denote a small domelike roof, a turret on a roof providing light, or the ceiling inside a dome.

Cushion capital A feature of Byzantine and Romanesque architecture, it consists of a rectangular block of stone with its lower corners rounded, resembling a cushion.

Decorated A word applied to a period in British architecture, following from Early English (q.v.), namely, from about 1300 to about 1375 (and later in some areas), in which the main feature is decorative treatment of windows (tracery), multiplication of ribs in vaulting (see **Vault**), giving intricate patterns, and the use of ogee arches (see **Arches**). The period is also noted for high clerestory windows.

Diaper Surface decoration consisting of squares or diamonds, incised or in shallow relief (especially on columns in Durham).

Drum Cylindrical or polygonal ring of walling that supports a dome.

Early English The opening period of British Gothic architecture, dating from about 1180 to about 1300. It is characterized by the first tall lancet windows (q.v.) and steeply pointed arches, and clusters of slender shafts replacing earlier Romanesque columns.

Egg-and-dart moulding A decorative motif on moulding in the form of alternate egg and dart.

Elevation The vertical aspect of a building, or part of a building.

Façade The front of a building.

Fan vaulting See **Vault**.

Fluting A parallel series of straight semicircular channels on a surface, especially on a column.

Flying buttress Stone buttress in the form of an arch acting as a prop, its upper part resting against the high main wall of a nave, transept or choir, its lower end resting against a pier, to absorb outward thrust.

Foliated Decorated with leaflike patterns.

Fresco Painting on walls or ceilings done in watercolours while the plaster is still wet.

Galilee porch A porch at the west end of a cathedral, all or part of which is used as a chapel. The name comes from the Latin *galeria*, a long porch, though it is also held to derive from the Sea of Galilee in Palestine.

Gothic (See Introduction.) The word 'Gothic' was used by the Italian painter and historian, Giorgio Vasari (1511–74), to describe the architecture of the 12th to 15th centuries in Europe which he and his contemporaries regarded as barbaric because it ignored Classical purity and truth. The Goths were peoples who overran parts of the Western Roman Empire in the 5th century.

Greek cross A cruciform plan where the four arms are of equal length.

Groin vault See **Vault**.

Hall church A rectangular church in which the nave and aisles are of the same height, and which therefore has neither triforium nor clerestory.

Iconostasis A screen in an Eastern cathedral, on which icons are placed, which divides the east end from the rest of the building.

Kokoshniki Arches (usually over panels or windows) set in rows as decoration. The term derives from

Ground plan of a typical basilica, Trogir Cathedral in Yugoslavia. The principal parts are numbered as follows:
1 Narthex
2 Nave
3 Aisles
4 Apses

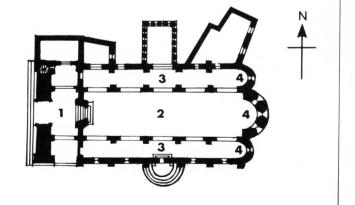

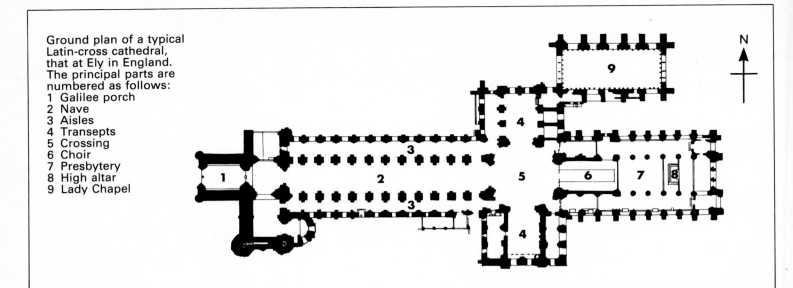

Ground plan of a typical
Latin-cross cathedral,
that at Ely in England.
The principal parts are
numbered as follows:
1 Galilee porch
2 Nave
3 Aisles
4 Transepts
5 Crossing
6 Choir
7 Presbytery
8 High altar
9 Lady Chapel

N

the Russian word for a type of
headdress worn by women (see St
Basil's, Moscow).

Lady Chapel Chapel dedicated to
the Virgin Mary, usually at the east
end.

Lancet A tall, narrow window,
sharply pointed.

Lantern An open turret on a dome
or tower, with windows.

Latin cross A cruciform plan
where the nave arm is longer than
the other three arms.

Lierne vault See **Vault**.

Light Once another word for a
window, now more usually for a
subdivision of a window.

Machicolation Projecting part of a
stone or brick parapet with holes or
slats in the floor.

Misericord A wooden bracket or
ledge underneath a hinged seat in a
choir, which when the seat is tipped
up provides support for someone
having to stand for long periods.
Misericords were often beautifully
carved.

Narthex The western porch end of
a cathedral of basilican plan.

Nave The western arm of a
cathedral or church.

Neoclassical Revived classical
styles of architecture.

Niche A shaped shallow recess in a
wall, pier or buttress, to house a
statue or an ornament.

Ogee arch See **Arches**.

Pediment The triangular low-
pitched gable end in Classical
architecture that crowns the front of
a building. The term was later used
to denote any triangular or curved

structure over a door or portico.

Pendentive A spherical triangular
block of masonry formed by the
intersecting of a dome by two pairs
of opposing arches which are carried
on piers or columns (see St Sophia's,
Istanbul).

Perpendicular The last (third)
period of British Gothic architecture,
of about 1370 to about 1480,
characterized by upright lines of
window bars, fan vaulting and wide
windows.

Pier A solid mass of stone, brick or
concrete walling between two
openings, designed to sustain vertical
pressure. It can be simple, that is,
round or rectangular, or compound,
that is, shaped in a mix of profiles
either solid or made up from a
cluster of shafts.

Pilaster A flat rectangular column
partly let into a wall or pier.

Pinnacle Slender, turretlike point
at the top of a buttress, roof or
parapet, decorated.

Plateresque Rich, surface
ornament characteristic of Spanish
architecture resembling gold or
silverwork.

Portal An elaborate doorway.

Presbytery Eastern end of a
cathedral. The term is sometimes
used to indicate the whole east end,
but more specifically the area east of
the choir stalls and before the high
altar. In cathedrals it is usually one
step or two higher than the choir.

Pulpitum A solid screen, generally
of stone, which shuts off the choir
from the nave. In many cases it has
a gallery above.

Reredos The screen at the back of
an altar, usually much decorated.

Retable A shelf behind and above
an altar, to hold the cross and other
ornaments.

Retrochoir Part of the cathedral
behind where the choir sits. It is
usually a walkway immediately east
of the high altar.

Rib A narrow projecting member
supporting or strengthening a panel
of a vault or ceiling.

Rococo A European decorative
style of the period *c.* 1690–*c.* 1760
characterized by light, assymetrical
patterns based upon scrolls and
shells.

Romanesque An architectural style
in Europe based on Roman models,
employed from the end of the 5th
century to the end of the 13th
century.

Rood screen An ornamental screen
of wood, with openwork above
panelling. In some cathedrals it takes
the place of a pulpitum.

Rose window Large circular
window decorated with tracery and
stained glass.

Rosette A rose window, or a rose-
shaped decoration.

Rotunda A building of circular
ground plan surmounted by a dome.
Also another word for a dome.

Sacristy Room adjoining or part of
a cathedral where sacred vessels and
garments are kept.

Sanctuary See **Presbytery**.

Splay foot Having the broad foot
turned outwards.

Star or stellar vaulting See **Vault**.

Stucco Plaster coated on a wall
surface or moulded into architectural
decoration or sculpture.

Tracery Ornamental stonework in
the top parts of a Gothic window.

Transepts In a cruciform church
or cathedral, the transverse arms
running north to south between the
choir and the nave. Some cathedrals
have a second, more easterly, pair of
transepts, such as at Durham and
Salisbury.

Triforium An arcaded wall
passage below the clerestory and
above the nave arcades (and
continuing round the transepts and
choir in some cathedrals).

Tympanum The space, often
triangular, above the lintel and
beneath the enclosing arch of a
doorway. It is usually decorated.

Vault The arched covering, in
stone, wood or brick, of a building.
There are several types of vaulting:
  Barrel vault: continuous vault in
  cylindrical section, like a tunnel.
  Fan vault: vault whose ribs spring
  out of a column and spread
  fanwise.
  Groin vault: where individual
  vaults cross each other at right
  angles.
  Lierne vault: a vault incorporating
  short, intermediate cross ribs,
  producing intricate patterns.
  Stellar, or star, vault: vaulting
  where the ribs converge into a
  starlike pattern.

Voussoir A stone or brick wedge-
shaped component of an arch.